SIMPLY SUPER PAPER

SIMPLY SUPER PAPER

Over 50 Projects to Cut, Curl, Twist, and Tease from Paper

SANDRA LOUNSBURY FOOSE

CB
CONTEMPORARY BOOKS

Library of Congress Cataloging-in-Publication Data

Foose, Sandra Lounsbury.
    Simply super paper : over 50 projects to cut, curl, twist, and tease
from paper / Sandra Lounsbury Foose.
        p.   cm.
    ISBN 0-8092-2864-5
    1. Paper work.   I. Title.
TT870.F64   1999
745.54'393—dc21
                                                            98-46895
                                                                CIP

Warning: When using cutting tools and other suggested products, readers are strongly cautioned to follow manufacturers' directions, to heed warnings, and to seek prompt medical attention for any injury. In addition, readers are warned to keep all potentially harmful supplies away from children.

The TABASCO® marks, bottle and label designs are registered trademarks and servicemarks exclusively of McIlhenny Co., Avery Island, LA 70513.

Editorial and production direction by Anne Knudsen
Art direction by Kim Bartko
Project editing by Blythe Smith
Cover and interior design by Mary Lockwood
Cover and interior photography by Sharon Hoogstraten
Drawings by Sandra Lounsbury Foose

Published by Contemporary Books
A division of NTC/Contemporary Publishing Group, Inc.
4255 West Touhy Avenue, Lincolnwood (Chicago), Illinois 60712-1975 U.S.A.
Copyright © 2000 by Sandra Lounsbury Foose
All rights reserved. No part of this book may be reproduced, stored in a retrieval system,
or transmitted in any form or by any means, electronic, mechanical, photocopying, recording,
or otherwise, without the prior written permission of NTC/Contemporary Publishing Group,
Inc., with the following limited exception. The reader may photocopy the templates on
pages 89 to 132 in order to use them to make the projects for his/her personal use.
Commercial use of this publication and its contents is strictly prohibited.
Printed and bound in Hong Kong by Midas Printing Company
International Standard Book Number: 0-8092-2864-5

25 24 23 22 21 20 19 18 17 16 15 14 13 12 11 10 9 8 7 6 5 4 3 2 1

For Mom and Dad,
with loving thoughts,
and a heart full of happy memories,
especially the snowflakes.

Contents

Preface

A gift of paper is often the first art material placed in the hands of a child—a box of eight fat crayons being the second. The box is opened. Crayon meets paper. The first timid lines lead to joyous scribbles and then thick patches of waxy color. So begins the medley of discovery and delight.

In time, paper and child are introduced to pencils, scissors, all kinds of glue, and brushes dripping with paint. One bright idea leads to another until the day when simply paper, varying in texture, weight, and hue, is seen as a wonderful gift all by itself, a magical source of creative possibility and play. Cut and curled, rolled, wrinkled, folded or fringed, even torn into tiny bits, paper is fun, it's affordable, it's forgiving, and best of all, it's everywhere!

Paper becomes less of a playmate and more of a workmate or a helpmate as the years pass by. At work each day, in so many ways, paper touches our lives and we, in turn, touch paper. There are books, newspapers, schedules, notes, instructions, exams, licenses, certificates, notices, ballots, business cards, name tags, memos, reports, itineraries, programs, records, lists, announcements, diagrams, patterns, stamps, packages, tickets, money, invoices, checks, statements, receipts, and more.

At home, too, paper holds our dreams of tomorrow and our memories of yesterday in journals, scrapbooks, photographs, love letters, confetti, and children's precious drawings. Playmate, helpmate, or workmate, paper is a source of wonder and can also be a means of creative expression all through our lives.

There is something magical about taking an ordinary piece of paper in hand, transforming it with just a few quick cuts and folds, and giving it life in another form as a bird, or a basket, or a tree. When we intervene only a little, allowing the basic material to retain much of its own character, the results can be charming and sophisticated at one and the same time.

Children understand the magic of paper, because children know how to play, and paper inspires play. Actually, grown-ups *do* play with paper now and then, but most often when it provides an antidote to the boredom of a tedious meeting or a very dull sermon. This "playing" is well described by Robert Harbin in a passage from his 1957 origami book, *Paper Magic*: "How impossible it is to hold a small piece of paper in the fingers for any length of time without beginning to fiddle with it. Quite unconsciously the fingers will bend and roll and fold the paper, making it into some shape other than the original, even if the result is no more than a crumpled ball which is thrown away. The instinct is the same . . . but when a creative mind directs the fingers, a definite form will emerge, a model with meaning."

Let your creative mind wander through the pages and seasons of this book. Then look again at paper, that remarkable yet underappreciated material, take it in hand, and play!

ACKNOWLEDGMENTS

For their congeniality and their collaboration in bringing this book to life, I am extremely grateful to Sandra Taylor, my agent in Houston, and Anne Knudsen, executive editor at NTC/Contemporary Publishing Group. Many thanks to each of you for making a very big wish come true. My appreciation is also extended to Sanderson for providing the wallpaper samples used throughout the book.

SIMPLY SUPER PAPER

I
Getting
Started

GETTING STARTED

This part will be easy because you've already completed the course work for Paper Play 101. Just think of all those preschool and kindergarten years of cut-fold-paste as basic training. But in case you've forgotten, here's a quick review of supplies, tools, and techniques. Let's start with the fun stuff—the paper!

Discovering Paper

Art Paper: These high quality, heavy-weight papers are made by Canson, Crescent, Canford, Strathmore, Fabriano, and other manufacturers. Richly hued, subtly textured art papers are an inspiration to heart, eye, and hand. Unlike construction paper, which fades easily and splits when scored and folded, art paper holds its color and has good strength and memory. When art paper is scored and folded it will not crack or tear, and when it is curled and rolled it will keep its form.

Bond Paper: Available in white and a rainbow of wonderful colors, this is ordinary, inexpensive, stationery-weight paper, usually measuring 8½″ × 11″ (22.0 cm × 28.0 cm) in size. Fabulous colors with matching envelopes are often sold in copy shops.

Corrugated Cardboard: Since it is often used for protective packaging, sometimes you can rescue this textured paper from a recycling bin. Colored and metallic corrugated board, occasionally called corduroy paper, can be purchased in rolls as well as in individual sheets. When the corrugated texture is accidentally crushed, repair it by running a thin dowel or a bamboo skewer inside the tunnels and lifting up the dents.

Duplex Paper: This is a light- to medium-weight multipurpose paper with a different color on each side of a single sheet. Also known as duet paper, the duplex paper used in this book was made by Bemiss-Jason.

Foil Paper and Foil Board: Smooth and shiny or embossed with texture, metallic foil paper looks wonderful lining envelopes, and that's a great place to salvage it too! Working with brightly colored, high-gloss foil can be a bit rough on the eyes, especially at night, because of the glare created by artificial lighting. When you work with foil board, remember that once you score and fold it, the board beneath the foil surface will appear as a white line on your work.

Garden Paper: This soft, delightful, handmade paper is embedded with real flowers, leaves, and seeds, so no two pieces are ever alike. It is so lovely.

Glow-in-the-Dark Paper: Luminescent paper is kind of a splurge because of its price, but it sure is fun to use! It cuts and folds like origami paper and every time it is exposed to light, it will glow brightly for at least thirty minutes afterward.

Graph Paper: Select graph paper with boldly printed inch lines and a grid size of either four squares per inch (4×4) or eight squares per inch (8×8). If you need a large piece for pattern making, tape smaller pieces together after overlapping and aligning the squares.

Kraft Paper: Humble but handsome and easy to salvage, kraft paper is most often used for bagging groceries and wrapping parcels, because of its strength and low cost. Now and then you may encounter kraft paper enhanced with a printed design or brushed with a metallic wash, and the look is surprisingly elegant.

Lace Paper Doilies: Frosty white circles, squares, rectangles, ovals, and hearts of paper lace can be found in card shops, supermarkets, and places that sell party supplies.

Origami Paper: In addition to the familiar packages of brightly colored squares, origami paper is also available in metallic foil, double-sided, iridescent, luminescent, opalescent, and Japanese folk-art print assortments.

Vellum: A medium-weight, high quality, transparent paper, vellum is stronger than ordinary tracing paper. It makes interesting transparent envelopes that can actually be sent through the mail.

Velour Paper: Also known as flocked paper, velour paper has a soft, fuzzy, suedelike finish.

Wallpaper: Uncoated sheets of upscale wallpaper pulled from an old sample book were used to make several of the projects in this book. Wallpaper samples also make wonderful note cards, place mats, book covers, photo mats, and gift-wraps.

Collecting Scraps

Without spending a single penny you can create a fabulous paper palette from scraps, leftovers, and throwaways.

Gift-giving occasions yield wrappings and boxes, ribbons and strings, as well as the colorful paper of greeting cards, envelopes, and their linings. Packaging materials worth salvaging could be lurking just inside the shopping bags and other merchandise you regularly carry home. Even the mailbox holds potential treasures in the form of advertisements, invitations, annual reports, garden catalogs, promotional mailings, and such. Check for unusual colors, patterns, and textures on folders, bags, stationery, calendars, playing cards, newspapers, maps, the covers of old notebooks, damaged sheets of music, and even lightbulb cartons with their corrugated inserts.

Search your community for other freebie possibilities. Many of the patterned papers you will see in this book were found in a discontinued wallpaper sample book about to be discarded by an interior-design shop in my small town. Local printers might have outdated or duplicate paper sample books that could be yours for the asking. Usually these swatch books are also available at paper superstores and paper wholesalers. After carefully removing the samples from the books (watch those staples), you will often find that the swatches are large enough to make complete projects. In fact, nearly half the projects in this book were made with just such salvaged scraps.

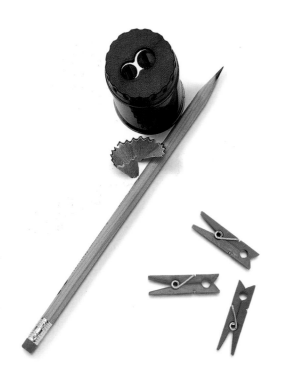

THE WORK BOX

Collect all of these pieces of basic equipment and stash them together in a big box, a sturdy basket, a tote bag, or a plastic storage container. For safety's sake, if there are little children in your home, be sure to keep your work box out of their reach. Every time you make a project you will need to use at least one item from your work box. Since you will have all these things stored together and close at hand, most of the items in the work box won't appear again on the materials list provided for each project.

Acetate: This strong, transparent material is used to make sturdy, long-lasting patterns. Although it can be purchased, it is very easy to scavenge acetate from packaging components such as gift box lids.

Brads: Traditional brass fasteners have a flexible shank that can be opened like two wings in order to join hole-punched pieces of paper.

Clip Clothespins: Clothespins are perfect for holding glued pieces of paper together while they dry. They also function as giant paper clips, keeping your patterns, papers, and notes organized.

Compass: An ordinary pencil-holding compass is all you need to draw accurate circles.

Cotton Swabs: When dampened just a little bit, a cotton swab is the perfect tool for removing glue spots. When all the cotton is pulled off a swab the remaining stick can become a part of a project, such as the perch on a Birdhouse Gift Box (page 37).

Craft Knife with Replacement Blades: Scissors can be used for some of the projects, but many involve delicate, precision cutting and require the use of a craft knife with a #11 blade. Select a knife with a soft, rubberized (preferably contoured) barrel for comfort and control, an antiroll device, and a cap for safety. The knife should also have a safe and easy blade release mechanism. The X-ACTO® X2000 knife has all of these features. In order to protect your most precious tools—your own two hands—avoid all other cutting devices. Children should not use craft knives.

Crochet Cotton, Pearl Cotton, Silky Cord, Thread, Ribbon, and String: Available in craft and fabric shops, these fiber materials are most often used to make hanging loops on ornaments or details on other projects.

Cutting Mat: Heavy cardboard can be used for a temporary cutting mat, but it will wear out very quickly and dull the blade of your craft knife. Self-healing rotary cutting mats are really made for rotary cutters, and they forget how to heal when a craft blade mars the surface. The very best resilient cutting base has a translucent, semihard, rubberlike surface that accepts the blade and then miraculously heals itself. The cutting mat, manufactured by Alvin, is nonslip, nonglare, and conveniently marked with a 1″ grid pattern. It heals so completely that I use it as both a drawing surface and a cutting surface. This is a pricey item, but worth the investment.

Erasable Tracing Paper: Used like carbon paper to transfer patterns, this is a waxless, greaseless, smudge-proof material. Graphite and white transfer paper are made in reusable 18″ × 36″ (45.0 cm × 90.0 cm) sheets and it's best to have one of each color.

Eraser: With gentle pressure, a nonabrasive white vinyl eraser removes pencil lines cleanly, without smudging. For precise work the most convenient form is an eraser that resembles a mechanical pencil and can also be refilled.

Felt Tip Pens: An inexpensive, basic set of fine-line felt-tip markers is adequate. Test markers on paper to check for feathering of color.

Glue: Nearly every project in this collection was made with an Elmer's All-Purpose Glue Stick (not the Craft Glue Stick or the School Glue Stick). White liquid Elmer's Glue-All™ was used for the rest of the projects. Both of these adhesives dry clear and make a strong bond. They also dry quickly, but not instantly, so if you work fast you can make small adjustments. Always try a test patch of glue on your good paper.

Monofilament: This soft, invisible, nylon sewing thread is used to make some of the ornament projects.

Needles and Pins: Needles and pins are most often used to pierce holes in patterns so construction details can be inconspicuously transferred onto your paper with tiny pencil dots. Occasionally pins and needles are used to make pierced design details directly on a project, so you should have a variety of sizes, some quite thin and some chunky. "T" pins are a good choice, because the "T" bar at the top serves as a little handle, making the pin easy to hold.

Paper Clips: These can be real time-savers when used to hold glued layers of paper together to dry. To avoid scratching your work, use paper clips with care and remove them promptly so they don't leave any rust marks.

Optional

Drawing Board: To make the projects in this book, a drawing board with T-square and triangles is not essential, but such supplies do ensure accuracy and efficiency. If you consider such a purchase, a white plastic Koh-I-Noor® Studio Drawing Board with a paper clamp and a removable transparent sliding straightedge acting as a T-square on it is affordable and more than adequate. To complete the set, use separately purchased inexpensive 6″ (15.0 cm) 30°/60° and 45°/90° plastic triangles on the board. Neither the plastic board nor the plastic triangles should be used with a craft knife.

The Essential Work Box

Clip clothespins

Compass

Cotton swabs

Craft knife and package of #11 replacement blades

Cutting mat, self-healing type or sheets of thick cardboard (not corrugated)

Erasable transfer paper, light and dark

Eraser, nonabrasive white vinyl

Elmer's All-Purpose Glue Stick

Elmer's Glue-All™ (white liquid glue)

Needles and pins

Paper clips

Pencil sharpener, very good quality, handheld type

Pencils with erasers for drawing; white pencil

Rulers, 6″ (15.0 cm) and 12″ (30.0 cm), or 18″ (45.0 cm)

Scissors, 7″ (18.0 cm) student or all-purpose; 5″ (12.0 cm) embroidery scissors

Straightedge, metal, 18″ (45.0 cm) or 24″ (60.0 cm)

Tape, transparent, and masking or removeable

Toothpicks, round type

Tracing paper pad

Tweezers

Water in small tightly sealed jar

Paper Punches: Metal plier-type paper punches are available in ⅛″ (0.3 cm), ³⁄₁₆″ (0.5 cm), and ¼″ (0.6 cm) diameters. All three sizes are used for projects in this book, but if you have trouble finding the ³⁄₁₆″ (0.5 cm) diameter, the ¼″ (0.6 cm) size could be substituted. Decorative paper punches are great for quickly producing a variety of cute confetti shapes, such as hearts, stars, and butterflies.

Pencil Sharpener: A quality handheld sharpener with a twist-off barrel to empty shavings will help keep your desk and your work neat.

Pencils: You will need a traditional #2 wooden school pencil with a soft graphite lead for tracing patterns and transferring patterns onto paper. A white coloring pencil is essential for transferring patterns onto dark paper.

Ruler: I like to work with flat metal rulers and use a 6″ (15.0 cm) and a 12″ (30.0 cm) for most projects. Consider purchasing a safety ruler, which can serve double duty as a measuring device as well as a straightedge when cutting with a craft knife. Safety rulers have nonskid backings and are especially designed so there is a barrier between your fingers and the knife.

Scissors: When selecting scissors, it is very important to consider comfort as well as size. Try them before you buy them. For general use I favor lightweight, all purpose, 7″ (18.0 cm) Fiskars® scissors, with molded plastic handles suitable for right-handed or left-handed use. For delicate and precise work I use 5″ (12.0 cm) pointed-tip embroidery scissors. Paper edgers are used for cutting decorative borders. Dozens of designs are available, but only the scallop and the zigzag edgers were used in this book.

Straightedge: A metal straightedge is required to safely cut paper with a craft knife. It must protect your fingers, so look for one with a nonskid backing and a barrier or a lip on one of its edges.

Tape: Transparent tape is occasionally used to hold paper pieces together and to reinforce delicate scoring lines. Masking tape is used when making patterns (removable tape can also be used for this purpose).

Toothpicks, Dowels, and Bamboo Skewers: These items are used as materials for some projects, like the pinwheels in Chapter 4, and as tools for others, most often when adding bits of glue in tight places. Select rounded toothpicks, not flat ones.

Tracing Paper: When you do not photocopy patterns, use this lightweight, transparent paper to trace the patterns directly from the book. Purchase an 8½″ × 11″ (20.0 cm × 28.0 cm) or a 9″ × 12″ (23.0 cm × 30.0 cm) pad. If you need a larger piece of paper, tape the small sheets together.

Tweezers: Use tweezers to move tiny pieces of paper into position and to hold hard-to-reach layers of paper together while drying.

Tricks & Techniques

"If all else fails, read the directions." I don't know who first offered that advice, but I know many who take it to heart! Granted, the best lessons do sometimes come from our worst mistakes. Generally speaking, however, taking the time to review basic information at the beginning of an activity is a better way to learn, so please read on.

Making Patterns: Some projects are best made with photocopied patterns, but most can be traced directly from the book. Hold the tracing paper in place on the page with paper clips or small pieces of masking tape applied with very light pressure. When you work quickly and use a gentle touch, masking tape can usually be lifted off the page with ease. To be sure that your tape can be removed without a trace, make a small test patch on an inconspicuous spot in the book. Strive for accuracy when tracing, because a well-made pattern will ensure the best results. Check your straight-sided patterns for precision by holding them against graph paper. On the patterns, continuous solid lines are always cutting lines, dotted lines show placement of a detail or another piece, and broken lines indicate fold lines. Label all patterns and keep them clipped together or tucked into separate envelopes.

To strengthen patterns or make very tiny ones easier to handle, glue the pieces to acetate before cutting them out. When using a craft knife, it is not always necessary to cut straight through the acetate. Sometimes you can just score it on the pattern line and then complete the job by breaking the acetate on the scored line.

Transferring Details: Pattern shapes and details can be transferred onto the project paper in several ways.

The first method involves using a needle or a pin to pierce the pattern details, such as faces and fold lines, before the pattern is placed on the project paper. The details can then be transferred directly onto the paper by placing a very sharp pencil inside the pattern holes.

Whenever using commercial transfer paper is the preferred method for a project, it is mentioned in the instructions. Transfer paper is usually very responsive to pressure, so draw gently over the pattern lines, but always test the product on a scrap of your good paper before you use it.

Maintaining Supplies

Treat your paper collection with care. Store the sheets flat. You can make a hinged storage portfolio for large papers by using tape to join two same-size pieces of cardboard together along one edge. Sort smaller pieces of paper by color in folders, bags, or envelopes, but before you squirrel them away, remove all traces of tape so the adhesive residue will not mar the texture or discolor the paper surface.

Rolling paper for storage is not a good idea, but if you absolutely must do it, roll the pieces very loosely and don't put rubber bands, tape, or paper clips on them. Instead, wrap a strip of scrap paper around the roll and use a piece of tape to attach the strip to itself. If paper is difficult to flatten after being rolled, gently re-roll it in the opposite direction.

Keep paper out of the sun and away from moisture and be sure your hands are very clean and dry before you touch it. Dust, fingerprints, and graphite smudges are difficult to remove; color fading is irreversible.

Although it is easier said than done, keep your work area neat and clean. Only set up the items you need for the project at hand and keep your supplies clean too. Replace the cap on the glue. Store your tapes in plastic bags to keep the edges clean. Wash your hands after using pencils and glue. Don't use your drawing board for a snack tray.

If you are unable to find erasable transfer paper, here's one more transfer method. After tracing the pattern from the book, cut out the pattern, flip it over, and redraw the details on the reverse side of the pattern, right on top of the original detail lines. Then flip the pattern over again so the right side of it faces you. Place the pattern on the paper of your choice. Draw around the pattern and transfer the details by drawing on top of the detail lines again.

Determining Paper Grain: Some projects specify that a certain edge of a pattern should be placed "with the grain" on the chosen paper. Machine-made papers usually have a grain, which is a built-in directional preference based on the arrangement of the paper fibers. This structural quality makes it easier to fold or tear paper in one direction than in the other, say top to bottom, rather than side to side. Creasing a paper with the grain makes the cleanest folding line. Folds made across or against the grain sometimes appear uneven and ragged. Several projects require that folds be made in both directions and when that occurs, scoring the paper before folding will help to ensure a good appearance. The easiest way to test a paper's grain is to bring two of its parallel edges together, bending the paper at the middle without folding it. Then release the bend, rotate the paper ¼ turn, and bring the remaining two parallel edges together. The paper will show more resistance to being bent in one direction than the other. The grain runs parallel to the edges that are easiest to bring together, so a fold made parallel to those edges would be made with the grain.

Using Tape: Masking tape, removable tape, or paper clips are used to hold patterns on the project paper. If masking tape is your choice, it should be pulled off within minutes because usually the longer it stays in place, the more difficult it is to remove. Keep in mind that most tape is extremely rough on wallpaper. It's always wise to start by making a test patch of tape on your good paper to see if it mars the surface or leaves a sticky residue.

Erasing Drawings: Rough erasing will mar or tear the surface of paper and remove the color or make shiny spots on others. Use a light touch when drawing patterns so you won't need to remove heavy lines. If you must use an eraser, make slow strokes in one direction, instead of scrubbing the area at top speed.

Cutting Paper: Practice cutting paper scraps with a craft knife and find the way to hold it that gives you the greatest control and comfort. Never let yourself become careless with craft knives and X-ACTO® blades.

To cut or score straight lines with a craft knife, always use a nonslip safety ruler or straightedge as a barrier between your fingers and the blade. When cutting or scoring curved lines, keep moving the paper, instead of the knife, and place your fingers away from the path of the blade. If working on a small piece of paper brings your hand too close to the knife, securely tape the small piece of paper onto a bigger piece of cardboard. Always keep your eyes and your full attention on the blade.

When you are cutting multiple duplicate shapes together, stack the papers and use tape or clips to hold each layer of paper securely to the next. If the layers are not bound together, they will shift as pressure is applied to the knife, and the results will be distorted shapes. When cutting through multiple layers of paper, it is safer to make several successive cuts with gentle pressure rather than trying to cut through all the layers with one heavy-handed pass of the knife. It is hazardous to use a dull blade or one with even a tiny piece of the tip broken off. These conditions diminish your control of the knife and they will ruin the paper, tearing it instead of cutting it. Before you throw out a used blade, carefully wrap it in masking tape and then dispose of it responsibly.

For the greatest accuracy when cutting curves with scissors, keep the scissors stationary, without moving the wrist as you move the paper into the cutting blades, instead of keeping the paper stationary and moving the scissors around it.

Scoring Folding Lines: It is easy to make a crisp fold on lightweight origami paper, but medium- and heavy-weight paper must be first scored in order to fold neatly. To score, move the craft knife along an accurately drawn folding line (broken line on pattern) making a very shallow groove in the paper without cutting through it. Within the groove, the knife breaks only the very top fibers of the paper, enabling it to fold with ease and precision. Use a metal safety straightedge whenever you score folding lines. When scoring curved lines, move the paper instead of the knife as you follow the line. Small pieces are easiest to score before they are cut out.

Some projects require scoring on the front of the piece; others need scoring on the reverse side. The instructions will tell you when and where to score. Paper is usually bent away from a scored line. When you see the term mountain fold, the folding line is marked and scored on the right side of the paper and then the paper is bent away from you to create the peak of an imaginary mountain. When you see the term valley fold, the folding line is marked and scored on the reverse side of the paper and then the paper is flipped over to the right side and bent toward you to make a little valley. To create an accordion-folded piece of paper, make alternating parallel mountain and valley folds on it. To protect your paper, use a cover sheet of tracing paper over your work when creasing or flattening it. Be especially careful when scoring and folding wallpaper, because it may crack. If this happens, mend or reinforce a weak area by placing a piece of transparent tape on the reverse side of the trouble spot.

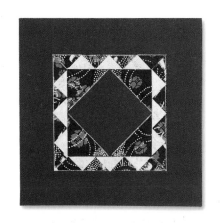

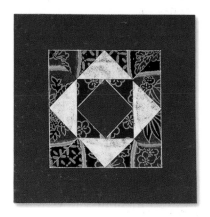

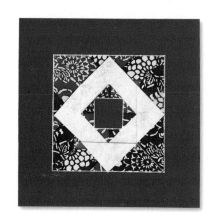

Curling and Curving Paper: When planning to curl paper strips, be sure to cut them with the grain of the paper and not across it. That is, the grain of the paper should run parallel to the long edges of the strips. In order to curl or curve a piece of paper, it is necessary to compress the fibers on one side of the piece while stretching them on the reverse side. Use a pair of closed scissors to curl small, lightweight or medium-weight pieces of paper. Hold one end of the strip firmly in one hand. Then starting from the point where the strip is being held and sandwiching the paper between the thumb of your other hand (on top) and the scissors (underneath), pull the closed scissors along the strip in one continuous motion. Your thumb (applying pressure to control the movement of the paper) and the scissors should travel together as the paper strip slides between them. If the scissors don't feel comfortable in your hand, try the edge of a ruler instead. For even more tightly curled paper, roll the curled strip around a bamboo skewer or a dowel.

A larger piece of paper can be curved by placing opposite ends of the piece in opposite hands and then pulling the paper back and forth over the edge of a tabletop or countertop. The table edge should be angular, not rounded. The table-edge method helps when making a cone, too. After using a pattern to cut out the cone shape, you can relax the paper a bit and give it a head start by running the widest part of the cone over the edge of the table. When making a cone, have a "rehearsal" with the piece before applying the glue. Use your fingers to gently roll the point area, coaxing it to curl without cracking the surface of the paper. Then roll the paper in one hand while twisting it tightly with the other hand. Coax the piece into a cone form and then release it. Apply the glue as directed, form the cone, and hold it until dry.

Interlocking Pieces: When joining some project pieces, a slot is cut a little more than halfway into each piece and then one slot is pushed into the other in order to lock the pieces together. A touch of glue is sometimes added to reinforce the union.

Adding Glue: Sometimes glue can change the color of the paper, or bubble its surface, so always make a glue test patch on the paper of your choice, and allow it to dry thoroughly before you proceed. Spread a thin layer of glue quickly and uniformly, using a pin, a toothpick, a popsicle stick, or a folded index card as a tool, depending on the size of the work. After joining glued surfaces, place a clean sheet of tracing paper (a cover sheet) over the work to protect it, and then rub the area to smooth it and distribute the glue. Do the smoothing with your fingertips, or roll a glue-stick tube on it, or pull your straightedge over the joint. Then remove the cover sheet and use paper clips or clothespins to hold the layers of the glued area together until dry. Alternatively, if the piece is flat, sandwich it between two layers of tracing paper and place it under a stack of heavy books until it is dry. Both Elmers' All-Purpose Glue Stick and Elmer's Glue-All™ will dry clear, but they might leave shiny spots on your work. If so, use a damp, not wet, cotton swab to carefully wipe away the dried glue. Keep the opposite cotton end dry so it can be used to smooth the dampened area and absorb excess moisture. First try the dampened swab on a scrap piece and you will see if moisture mars the paper surface or causes the color to bleed. Sometimes it's just better to leave the glue spot. Transparent tape should not be used in place of glue because it discolors, becomes brittle, and loses its adhesive quality with age.

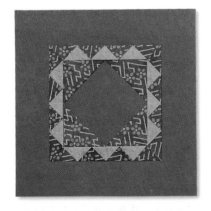

Mail-Order Catalogs

If you request all of these catalogs, you will be able to find just about everything used in this book. Call the toll-free numbers first because there might be a charge for some of the catalogs. Also, ask about the return policy of each company.

Dick Blick Art Material
Department SF
P.O. Box 1267
Galesburg, IL 61402-1267
1-800-828-4548

Home-Sew Sewing and
   Craft Supplies
P.O. Box 4099
Bethlehem, PA 18018-0099
1-800-344-4739
Fax: 610-867-9717

Kate's Paperie
561 Broadway
New York, NY 10012
1-888-941-9169

NASCO Arts and Crafts
East of the Rockies:
901 Janesville Avenue
Fort Atkinson, WI 53538-0901
1-800-558-9595
West of the Rockies:
4825 Stoddard Road
Modesto, CA 95356-9318
1-800-558-9595

Sax Arts and Crafts
P.O. Box 510710
New Berlin, WI 53151
1-800-558-6696
www.saxarts.com

2
Petals

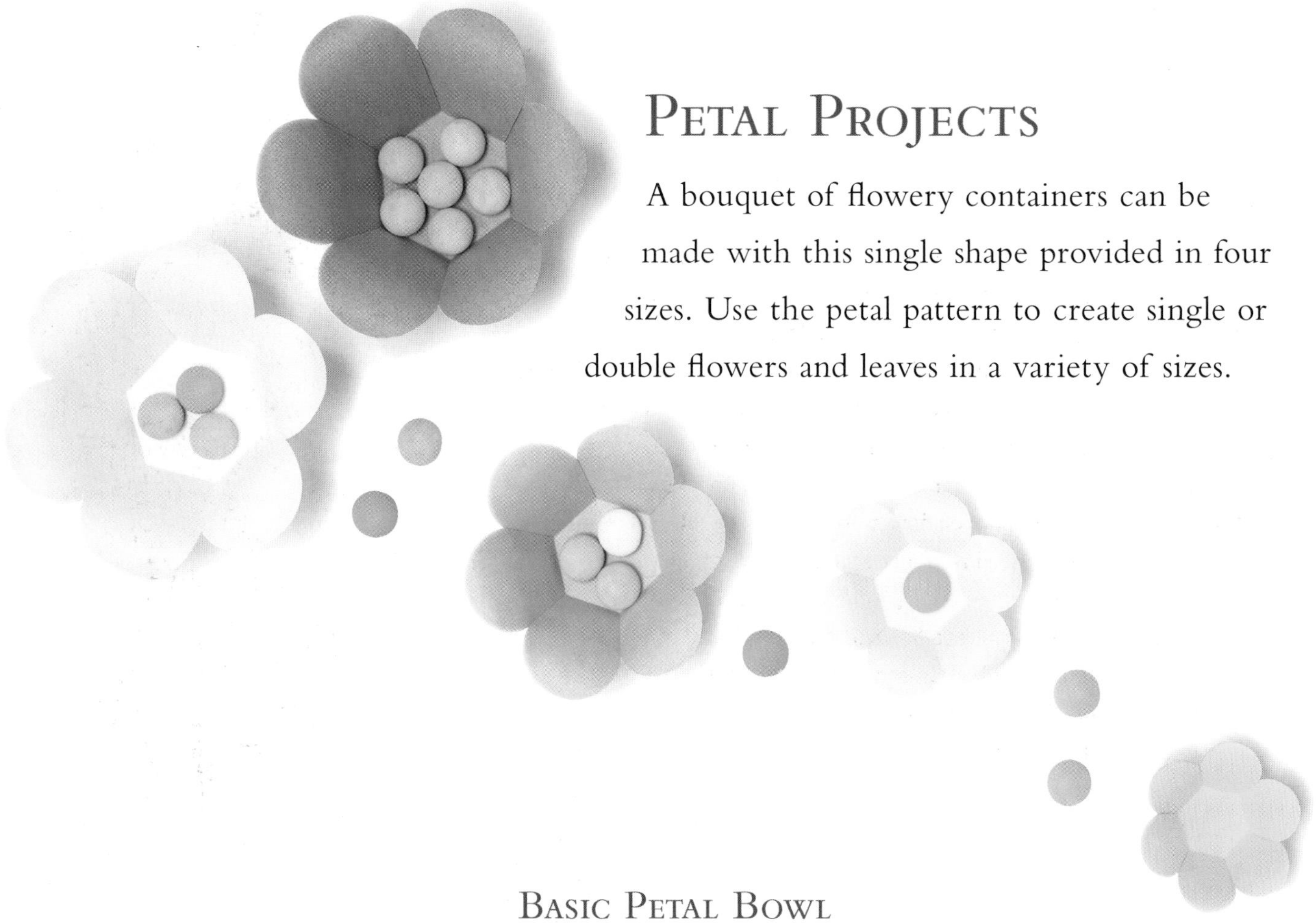

PETAL PROJECTS

A bouquet of flowery containers can be made with this single shape provided in four sizes. Use the petal pattern to create single or double flowers and leaves in a variety of sizes.

BASIC PETAL BOWL

General Instructions

1. Photocopy or trace pattern copying all details. Cut out pattern. Pierce pattern with needle pushed through every corner of center hexagon.

2. Tape or clip pattern onto paper surface that you want to be outside finished unit and use sharp pencil to draw around outside edge. Place tiny pencil dot in each pierced dot around center hexagon. Remove tape and hold pattern in place while completing outline. Remove pattern. Using very light pencil lines, connect dots to mark hexagon, folding lines, and cutting lines.

3. Cut out shape using craft knife and straightedge on protected work surface. Score each folding line and cut straight solid lines as indicated on pattern.

4. Fold up all petals on score lines around hexagon base of basket. Fold glue tab on each petal. See specific instructions below before gluing.

Materials

For one Petal Bowl unit, flower, or leaf

. . . .

Patterns on page 92

Equipment in work box, pages 4-6

6" (15.3 cm) square of sturdy paper for flowers

Green paper for leaves (refer to specific project for size)

Petal Basket

Refer to general instructions 1–4. For small basket, use pattern A
to cut one flower and pattern B to cut green leaves. Also cut ¼″ ×
7½″ (0.6 cm × 19.0 cm) green paper strip for handle. For medium
basket use pattern B to cut one flower and pattern C to cut green leaves.
Also cut ⅜″ × 9″ (1.0 cm × 22.8 cm) green paper strip for handle. For
large basket, use pattern C to cut one flower and pattern D to cut green
leaves. Also cut ½″ × 10″ (1.3 cm × 25.4 cm) green paper strip for
handle. Place glue tabs outside flower unit. Place glue tabs inside leaf
unit. Glue handle in place inside leaf portion of basket on
two opposite leaves. Short cut-edges of handle should rest
on hexagon base. Apply glue to hexagon base of flower
unit. Place flower unit inside leaf unit and twist flower
unit so midpoint of each petal is topped with
crevice formed by two adjacent leaves.

Pedestal Bowl

Refer to general instructions 1–4, cutting one
bowl in flower color and another of same size in
leaf color. Place glue tabs outside flower bowl. Place glue
tabs inside leafy pedestal. Glue flower on top of pedestal.

Gardenia Bowl

Refer to general instructions 1–4. Use pattern A to
cut one white flower, pattern B to cut one white
flower, and pattern C to cut one white flower. Place
all glue tabs outside flowers. Use pattern D to cut
one green leaf unit. Place glue tabs inside unit.
Apply glue to hexagon base outside of each flower
unit, but do not put glue on leaf unit. Starting with
smallest flower, place one inside other, twisting
flower so midpoint of each petal is topped with
crevice formed by larger unit around it.

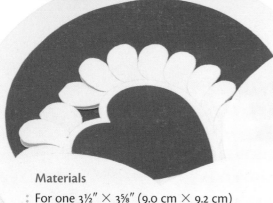

Materials

For one 3½" × 3⅝" (9.0 cm × 9.2 cm) card, ornament, or frame

Patterns on page 93

Equipment in work box, pages 4-6

4" × 8" (10.2 cm × 20.4 cm) piece of sturdy white paper

2½" (6.4 cm) square of red paper for center heart, optional

1¼" × 5" (3.2 cm × 12.8 cm) piece of sturdy white paper for frame easel, optional

16" (40.6 cm) length of fine red string for stitched card or ornament

11" (28.0 cm) length of string for ornament hanging loop

Envelope, 4¼" × 5⅛" (10.8 cm × 13.0 cm), or Envelope C pattern and instructions in Appendix, pages 88-91

FEATHERED HEARTS

A quilter's Feathered Heart motif provided the design for these three simple gifts. This single pattern will help you to make note cards, ornaments, and even little stand-up picture frames.

NOTECARD

Instructions

1. Photocopy or trace Feathered Heart pattern, but don't cut it out. If pattern has been photocopied, trim away excess paper around it.

2. Working with craft knife on protected work surface, score and fold white paper in half to make 4" (10.2 cm) square card. Aligning top edges, place 4" (10.2 cm) square of transfer paper on folded card, transfer surface facing down. Align "place on fold" edge of pattern on folded edge of card and clip in place. Trace over pattern lines and transfer dots too. Do not transfer easel placement line onto card. Remove pattern and transfer paper, but leave clips in place. Cut out unit around scalloped heart shape, but not between individual feathers. Cut out and discard crevice at heart top. Lightly score heart-shaped broken line at base of feathers.

3. Open card so it is flat. On front, cut between individual feathers. This cutting presents special hazards to fingers, so do it with great care.

4. Embellish heart in one of the following ways:

   Red Heart Card: Trace pattern for small center heart and cut out. Draw and cut out one red heart. Center and glue heart in place on card. Gently erase feathers if necessary.

   Pierced Heart Card: On card front only, use darning needle to pierce dots in center of heart. Gently erase.

   Stitched Heart Card: On card front only, use darning needle to pierce dots at center of heart and gently erase. Thread sewing needle with 16" (40.6 cm) piece of string. Starting at bottom, pass needle from front to back, leaving 3" (7.6 cm) of string extended outside of card front. Stitch card carefully so string loops won't catch on feathers. Leave 3" (7.6 cm) string extended outside card front when stitching is completed. Tie ends in bow and trim.

Glue only here. ↘

Fold and glue easel (side view).

PICTURE FRAME

On card front, connect dots to draw cutting lines for heart opening. Cut out heart shape to make frame. Place heart opening of frame in best position on photograph of your choice and use sharp pencil to very lightly draw within heart opening. Cut out photo ⅛" (0.3 cm) beyond outline. Glue edges of photo in place behind opening in frame. Trace and cut out pattern for easel. Draw one easel on white paper and cut out. Score and fold broken lines so profile resembles drawing when viewed from side. Glue tiny tab inside easel and allow to dry. Glue easel on back of frame with dot at center of easel's lower edge touching lowest crevice of scallops around heart (see pattern). Place one finger inside easel and flatten base to make frame stand.

PIERCED HEART ORNAMENT

Complete steps 1 and 2 of instructions for notecard, but leave card folded as you start step 3 so feathers will be cut on both front and back of card. Use darning needle to pierce dots through both paper layers. Score heart at base of feathers on both front and back of card. Pull end of 11" (28.0 cm) piece of string through crevice at heart top and tie ends in bow. Glue center layers of card together, if you wish.

On each side of ornament, gently fold feathers forward and crease slightly along scored line on heart. Pull feathers apart separately so they make a butterfly effect around edge of heart when ornament is viewed from side.

Heart Basket

Ready to fill with flowers or potpourri, this simple basket is made in one piece with an applied handle. Depending on your choice of colors, this little valentine can be used for weddings, anniversaries, and other celebrations of the heart.

Materials

For one 3″ × 3⅜″ (7.6 cm × 8.6 cm) basket, approximately 3¾″ (9.5 cm) high

Patterns on page 93

Equipment in work box, pages 4-6

8½″ × 9½″ (21.6 cm × 24.2 cm) piece of acetate, optional

8½″ × 9½″ (21.6 cm × 24.2 cm) piece of sturdy paper

Instructions

1. Trace or photocopy patterns for basket and handle with all details. Glue pattern to acetate if you wish and cut out. Pierce folding lines in several places with pin.

2. Place patterns on paper and anchor with paper clips or tape. Trace around outside edges. Push pencil into pinholes to transfer folding lines. Using craft knife and straightedge on protected work surface, cut out basket and score folding lines including glue tabs. Cut out handle and cut into ends as indicated on pattern.

3. Sharply crease basket on all scored folding lines. Apply glue to tab A at tip of heart. Fold up basket sides. Edge A overlaps tab A. Hold until dry. Apply glue to tab B at heart crevice. Edge B overlaps tab B. Hold until dry. Pull all short glue tabs outside basket and glue to base. Glue ends of handle inside basket at crevice and tip.

QUILT-BLOCK VALENTINE

An eight-pointed star block centered within a heart makes this foldout valentine perfect for a quilt-loving friend. Duplex paper, with a different color on each side, is the best choice for this project, as it provides contrast between the folded layers.

Instructions

1. Trace or photocopy both pattern sections. If patterns are photocopied, trim on outlines to 4″ × 8″ (10.2 cm × 20.4 cm). Tape pattern sections together at center as shown in Drawing 1.

2. Accuracy is especially important when making patterns for this project. Carefully cut out heart on panel 1, square on panel 2, and star on panel 3. Refer to Drawing 2 in order to cut and form open square at center of panel 4. Check for alignment of shapes by referring to Drawing 3 and accordion-folding pattern into card format. Fold panel 1 on top of panel 2. Fold panel 2 over panel 3 and then panel 3 over panel 4. If edges of card or cutouts don't align, make adjustments.

3. Tape duplex paper to work surface. Color for card front should face work surface. Inside color of card should face you. Tape pattern on paper. Using very sharp pencil, draw within each opening and indicate folding lines with pinholes. Remove pattern. Cut out heart, square, and star. On panel 4 cut X, and score and fold edges referring to Drawing 2. Score folding lines marked with pinholes. Fold card so heart is on front.

Materials

For one 4″ (10.2 cm) square card

Pattern on page 94

Equipment in work box, pages 4-6

4″ × 16″ (10.2 cm × 40.6 cm) piece of lightweight duplex paper

Envelope, 4¼″ × 5⅛″ (10.8 cm × 13.0 cm), or Envelope C pattern and instructions in Appendix, pages 88-91

---

panel 1	*panel 2*	*panel 3*	*panel 4*
♡	◇	✦	⊠

1. Join pattern sections together. This is inside of card.

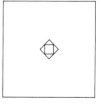

2. Create open square on panel 4 by cutting X and folding back each edge on score line.

3. Accordion-fold panels to create quilt block.

No-Glue Gift Box

Here is a pattern for a small no-glue gift box along with a suggestion for making a larger one. Any paper will do, but these boxes are especially pretty to make with scraps of fine wallpaper. You can make your own paper ribbon for the boxes too, by cutting strips of wallpaper or border with decorative-edge scissors. The paper ribbons can be tucked around just the box lid or used as a slide-on band around the entire box. When making the paper ribbon, use graph paper to determine the best width to cut and the best place to score it for folding at the box corners. Oh yes, and you will need some glue to attach the ribbons to the box.

Materials

For one 3½″ × 1″ (9.0 cm × 2.5 cm) square box or one 5″ × 1½″ (12.8 cm × 3.8 cm) square box

Patterns on pages 95-96

Equipment in work box, pages 4-6

Two 8″ (20.4 cm) square pieces of paper for small box

Two 11½″ (29.2 cm) square pieces of paper for large box

Four 5″ (12.8 cm) diameter paper doilies to line large box, optional

Note: Both base and lid will be cut, scored, folded, and assembled in same manner. However, center square and, therefore, overall dimensions of base unit are intentionally ⅛″ (0.3 cm) smaller than lid unit so that box top and bottom will fit together well. Before using good paper you may wish to make a practice piece or fold pattern to better understand assembly techniques.

Instructions

1. If making small box, trace or preferably photocopy patterns for box lid and base. If tracing, remember that accuracy is especially important when making this project. Mark all cutting lines and folding lines and label lid and base. If making larger box, enlarge small box lid and base patterns 43% on photocopier.

2. Working on protected surface with craft knife and straightedge, cut out patterns. Make four cuts on solid lines of each piece, as indicated on patterns and Drawing 1. Score all pattern folding lines. Crease on scored lines, making all mountain folds. Unfold each piece.

3. Tape or clip papers together on work surface in this order: selected paper, right-side up; transfer paper, right-side down; pattern, right-side up. Use pencil to very lightly draw on and around pattern, transferring all details. Remove pattern and transfer paper and reserve for another use. Leave selected paper right-side up on work surface. This surface will be on outside of box. Referring to Drawing 1 again, make four cuts on solid lines, as indicated on pattern and illustration. Also score and crease all folding lines, making mountain folds. Unfold unit completely.

4. Looking at Drawing 2, flip paper over to reverse side (inside of box) and for reinforcement, place tape, as shown, at end of each cut line.

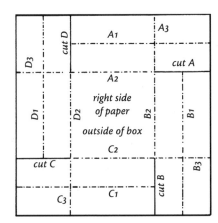

1. On right side of paper (outside surface of box), cut four solid lines A, B, C, D. Score all folding lines and make mountain folds. Unfold completely.

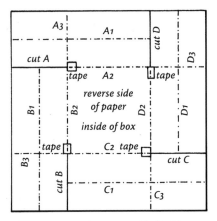

2. Flip paper over to reverse side (inside surface of box). Place piece of tape at end of each cut line A, B, C, D.

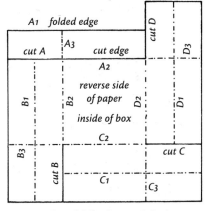

3. Crease along folding line A1, bringing cut edge of paper to meet folding line A2.

5. Referring to Drawing 3, crease along folding line A1, bringing cut edge of paper to align with folding line A2. If, instead, cut edge of paper overlaps folding line A2, trim edge of paper slightly. Rotate paper ¼ turn to right, and then crease folding line B1 so cut edge aligns with folding line B2. Make trimming adjustments if necessary and repeat rotating piece to fold and check sides C and D. Unit will resemble Drawing 4.

6. Referring to Drawing 5, raise side A into upright position to form one side of box along folding line A2. Then crease folding line A3, swinging excess paper down to form one corner of box. Rotate box ¼ turn to side B. Lift side B into upright position, open folding line B1, and then fold down side B, overlapping folded portion of side A that rests against it. This will lock corner of box. Crease folding line B3, and swing excess paper down to form another corner of box. Continue to fold all sides and corners as you did with side A. When you are ready to finish folding box sides, gently lift up flap of side A and carefully tuck final portion of side D under flap of side A.

7. If you wish to line base portion of large box with doilies, fold each doily in half across center. Place inside box so doily folding line aligns with top edge of box. It may be necessary to trim doily slightly if it does not fit well at corners (diameter may be a little too wide for box edge). Fit doily inside box, creasing doily to fit into bottom fold of base. Glue in place. Repeat to add remaining doilies. When dry, place gift in box, fold doilies over contents and overlap curved edges of lace at center.

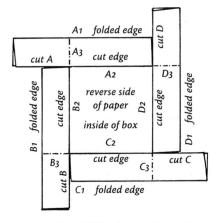

4. Crease along folding lines B1, C1, and D1.

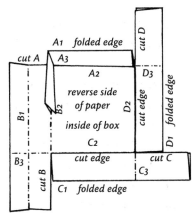

5. Fold box sides and corners and overlap edges.

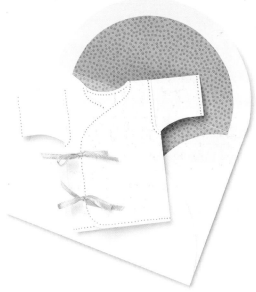

Baby Shirt Card

The cuteness of baby clothes is hard to resist. In hand they become tangible symbols of sweet treasured memories. This little note, styled like a tiny shirt, is just waiting to welcome a brand new baby.

Materials

For one 4″ × 5¼″ (10.2 cm × 13.4 cm) card

Pattern on page 97

Equipment in work box, pages 4-6

8½″ (21.6 cm) square of sturdy white paper

Paper punch, ⅛″ (0.3 cm) diameter circle

15″ (38.0 cm) length of narrow pastel ribbon

Fine-line felt-tip pen to match ribbon

Envelope, 4⅜″ × 5¾″ (11.2 cm × 14.6 cm), or Envelope B pattern and instructions in Appendix, pages 88-90

Instructions

1. Photocopy pattern, or trace it transferring all markings, and cut out. Use paper punch to cut two holes indicated on pattern. Pierce folding lines in several places with pin.

2. If you like one side of paper best, preferred surface should face you when placed on work surface. This will be outside of shirt when card is finished. Tape pattern to paper and trace around edge. Draw within punched holes and place pencil tip in pierced holes to transfer folding lines. Remove pattern. Using craft knife and straightedge on protected work surface, score all folding lines and cut out shirt.

3. Flip shirt so preferred side faces work surface, as in Drawing 1. Referring to Drawing 2, fold up lower portion and tuck sleeves through armholes. Close and overlap shirt front sections as in Drawing 3. If they don't close with ease, completely open card to resemble Drawing 1 again and slice little bits off the star-marked shirt sides, but not the sleeves. Close card again to resemble Drawing 3. If necessary, trim top edges across shoulders and make adjustments in neck area so all parts align. Glue two back layers (not front sections) together at shoulders.

4. To add topstitching design, first make test on paper scrap. Draw pencil line and then draw dots on it with felt pen. When dry, erase pencil line. Does pencil line disappear? Does ink smear or fade? Referring to photograph, lightly draw pencil guidelines approximately ¹⁄₁₆″ (0.2 cm) from edge around shirt front and back. Using fine-line pen, place evenly spaced tiny dots on these lines to suggest top stitching around shirt edges. Gently erase pencil guidelines. Use paper punch to cut holes. Cut ribbon into two same-sized pieces and tie one piece in each hole.

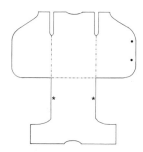

1. Flip over shirt to reverse side.

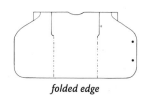

folded edge

2. Fold lower portion up and over upper portion. Tuck sleeves through armholes.

3. Close and overlap front sections.

BABY SHOE BASKETS

Embellish a shower table, accessorize a gift certificate, trim a present, or tether a bunch of balloons with these sweet little baby shoes. Cut from plain or patterned paper, they look cute when filled with potpourri, a few flowers, or candy treats.

Instructions

1. Trace shoe and sole patterns. To make insole pattern, trace around dotted lines inside sole pattern. Cut out patterns. Use pin to pierce placement line for glue tab on shoe and pierce center-front and center-back dots on shoe and sole.

2. Tape shoe pattern on paper, trace shape and place pencil in pattern holes to transfer center-front and center-back dots, as well as placement lines for glue tab on shoe. Flip shoe pattern over and trace another shoe in reverse. After removing pattern from work, lightly draw glue tab line on shoe. Also draw continuous line at top of tabs around lower edge of shoe to provide guideline for scoring. Draw two sole pieces and two insole pieces. Use pencil to transfer center front and center back dots.

3. Using craft knife on protected work surface, cut out shoe pieces. First cut around outer edge of tabs with knife or scissors. Then use knife along lower edge of shoe piece, making one continuous line but changing pressure on knife so you will be alternately scoring top of tabs and cutting edge of shoe between tabs as you work. Finally, cut along sides of tabs and remaining edges of shoe pieces. Punch out holes if using brads. Also cut out soles and insoles.

4. On one shoe piece, spread glue on right side of side glue tab. Bring side area with strap around so it overlaps side glue tab and forms a ring. Hold until dry. Turn shoe upside down. Working from bottom, hold insole inside shoe so wrong side faces you. Fold down center-front and center-back glue tabs, overlapping insole. Use tiny pieces of transparent tape to attach these two tabs to insole. Tape remaining tabs to insole. Place shoe flat on work surface. Using pencil with broken tip inside shoe, run it around edge of insole to flatten it against glue tabs.

5. Spread glue on sole. Working from bottom, apply sole to insole, sandwiching glue tabs in between layers. When glue has dried, look for places where sole extends beyond shoe and carefully trim away excess. Insert brad or glue strap and button in place. Repeat to finish other shoe.

Materials

For one pair of 1¾″ × 3¼″ (4.5 cm × 8.3 cm) shoes

Patterns on page 98

Equipment in work box, pages 4-6

6″ × 7½″ (15.3 cm × 19.0 cm) piece of acetate, optional

8½″ (21.6 cm) square piece of paper for shoes

4″ (10.2 cm) square piece of paper for insoles

4″ (10.2 cm) square piece of paper for soles

Two brads with ⅜″ (1.0 cm) shanks or small buttons

PHOTOGRAPH PORTFOLIO

For a quick and pretty way to protect, send, and display a treasured photograph, make one of these miniature portfolios. Patterns are provided for two small sizes, but once you understand the technique, you can make these folders any size or proportion you desire. The portfolios pictured here are made from scraps of wallpaper.

Materials

For one 2¼" (5.8 cm) square portfolio or one 2½" × 3⅛" (6.4 cm × 8.0 cm) rectangle portfolio

Pattern on page 99

Equipment in work box, pages 4-6

3⅛" × 10" (8.0 cm × 25.4 cm) piece of sturdy paper

18" (45.8 cm) length of ⅛" (0.3 cm) wide ribbon

Four photo corners

Instructions

1. Photocopy portfolio pattern, or trace it marking folding lines and cuts for ribbon slots, and cut out.

2. Clip or tape pattern onto good paper and use a few pinholes to transfer folding lines and cuts onto paper. Remove pattern.

3. Working on protected work surface, use craft knife and straightedge to score folding lines. Cut ribbon slots. With right side on outside, fold portfolio on center score line. Unfold and then fold cut edges to center folding line. If portfolio doesn't close well, unfold it and slice off a little bit of cut ends that meet at center.

4. Unfold portfolio so reverse side faces you. Referring to Drawing 1, run ribbon across two center sections of paper strip, pulling one ribbon end through each slot with help from a pin. Adjust ribbon ends so they are even. Ribbon ends will be much longer than drawing indicates. Note placement of transparent tape on each side of each ribbon slot.

5. Referring to Drawing 1, spread narrow border of glue along X-marked edges of first and last panel. Place a little glue on ribbon as well. Referring to Drawing 2, fold over each cut-edge, almost covering ribbon at center and hold until dry with paper clips or clothespins. Place photo corners on picture, moisten corners, and center photograph on inside of portfolio.

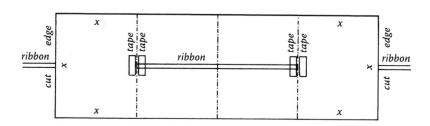

1. Tape ribbon and spread glue along X-marked edges.

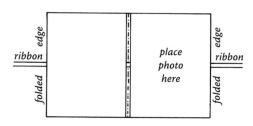

2. Fold cut edges toward center.

LACE EASTER EGG CARD

So often it seems that a mix of sweet memories inspires a creative response. Two happy thoughts of home, my mother's fondness for lace tablecloths and the way she tinted Easter eggs with only the palest of hues, blended in my mind's eye to become this delicate Easter greeting.

Instructions

1. Photocopy or trace card patterns, label, and cut out. Also cut out center egg shape. Write "place on fold" on proper edge of pattern. To make overlay pattern, trace along dotted lines shown on card pattern and trace egg at center. Cut out overlay and center egg shape. Overlay pattern should be 1/16" (0.2 cm) smaller than card pattern on all edges. Egg cutouts should be same size on both.

2. Using craft knife and straightedge on protected work surface, score and fold pastel paper in half crosswise. Along folded edge of paper, align edge of pattern marked "place on fold." Anchor pattern with masking tape and draw around shape. Draw within egg shape too. Cut out card and egg.

3. Tape and draw overlay piece on white paper. Cut out overlay piece and egg. Reserved egg shapes can be used for place cards or gift tags. On reverse side of overlay piece transfer centering dots at top, bottom, and sides.

4. Place overlay pattern on doily and move pattern around until you find best area. Cut portion of doily you wish to use, at least 1/4" (0.6 cm) larger than egg shape. Center doily (reverse side) in egg opening on reverse side of white overlay. Hold doily in place with a few pieces of tape. Place overlay on pastel card to see if lace placement pleases you. Make adjustments, if necessary, and then tape doily securely in place. Spread glue on pastel card to within 1/16" (0.2 cm) of edges. Align overlay on card, press together, and allow to dry while card is opened. Check around egg shape and around edges of overlay to see if any layers are separating. If so, add bits of glue with pin or toothpick.

Materials

For one 4⅛" × 5½" (10.5 cm × 14.0 cm) card

Pattern on page 100

Equipment in work box, pages 4-6

6" × 9" (15.3 cm × 23.0 cm) piece of sturdy pastel-colored paper

4½" × 6" (11.5 cm × 15.3 cm) piece of sturdy white opaque paper

Sections of lace paper doilies, preferably straight-edged or very large round or oval ones

Envelope, 4⅜" × 5¾" (11.2 cm × 14.6 cm), or Envelope B pattern and instructions in Appendix, pages 88-90

Note: For strength and opacity, don't separate layers of doilies individually. Instead, use two or three unseparated layers together.

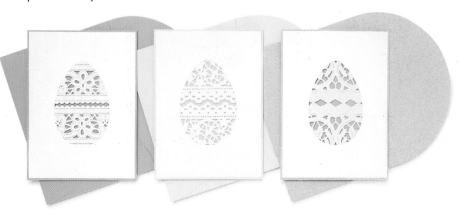

BUNNY NOTE AND GARLAND

A few folds, some quick snips, and presto! you can produce a bunny note card or a long garland parade of them. While equally cute cut in flowered or velour paper, this silhouette even looks good when cut from bunny-colored paper bags. To appeal to one's sense of touch as well as one's sense of humor, cut petal-covered bunnies from imported garden paper.

Materials

For one 3⅞″ × 4″ (9.8 cm × 10.2 cm) note

Large pattern on page 100

Equipment in work box, pages 4-6

4½″ × 8½″ (11.5 cm × 21.6 cm) piece of sturdy paper

Envelope, 4⅛″ × 5½″ (10.5 cm × 14.0 cm), or Envelope A pattern and instructions in Appendix, pages 88-90

Paper punch, ³⁄₁₆″–¼″ (0.5 cm–0.6 cm) diameter circle

Very narrow ribbon, 24″ (61.0 cm)

BUNNY NOTE

Instructions

1. Photocopy or trace pattern, and cut out. Use paper punch to cut out eye.
2. Score and fold paper in half crosswise to make 4¼″ × 4½″ (10.8 cm × 11.4 cm) card.
3. Align "place on fold" edge of pattern with folded edge of card and straight bottom edge of pattern with lower edge of card. Hold pattern in place with tape or paper clips. Draw around shape and within eye. Remove pattern.
4. Anchor folded card layers together with clips. Use craft knife on protected work surface to cut out bunny shape. Punch out eye.
5. Cut ribbon into two 12″ (30.5 cm) pieces. Tie one piece around neck of each bunny.

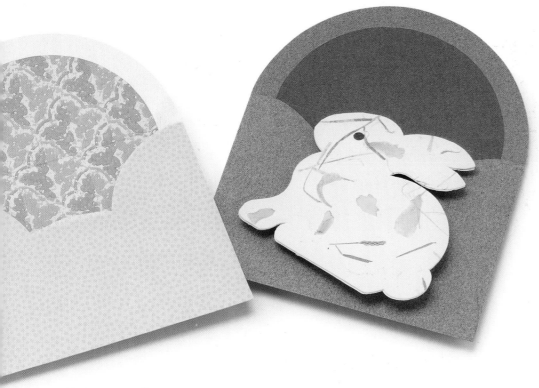

Bunny Garland

Instructions

1. Photocopy smallest bunny pattern, or trace it transferring facial details, and cut out. Punch out eye.

2. Cut 8½" × 11" (21.6 cm × 28.0 cm) paper into three 2¾" × 10" (7.0 cm × 25.4 cm) pieces. Fold each piece in half to 2¾" × 5" (7.0 cm × 12.8 cm). Open paper and bring each short cut-edge to meet at center fold and crease. Paper should have four equal sections divided by folding lines. Unfold paper and refold on same folding lines, making accordion (alternating mountain and valley) folds. Crease all folding lines sharply.

3. Place bunny pattern on folded paper. Edges of pattern should touch folded edges of paper. Tape or clip in place, draw around shape, and remove pattern.

4. Anchor folded paper layers together with tape or clips. Using craft knife on protected work surface, cut out bunny shape.

5. Repeat process to make additional sections of garland with remaining paper pieces and join together with transparent tape.

Materials

For three garland sections, each 2½" × 10" (6.4 cm × 25.4 cm) when unfolded

Small pattern on page 100

Equipment in work box, pages 4-6

8½" × 11" (21.6 cm × 28.0 cm) lightweight paper

Paper punch, ⅛" (0.3 cm) diameter circle

Note: If paper does not fold well, it may be necessary to score it before folding.

3
Sunshine

PAGE CORNER BOOKMARKS

These quick-to-cut bookmarks are made to hug page corners, and their toylike shapes and crayon-bright colors make leisure reading more fun than ever.

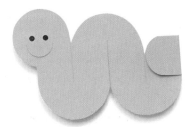

BOOKWORM BOOKMARK

Instructions

1. Trace pattern, but don't cut it out. Place transfer paper between tracing paper and green paper. Hold paper layers together with tape or clips.
2. Draw on top of pattern lines. Remove pattern and transfer paper.
3. Use craft knife on protected work surface to cut out bookworm. Cut on mouth line and into body crevices. Score glue tabs.
4. Fold down top glue tab and then cover it with glue tab folded from side. If necessary, trim glue tabs to align properly. Glue side tab to top tab to form corner pocket. Draw black eyes on head on each side of bookworm.

Materials

For one 1½″ × 2½″ (3.8 cm × 6.4 cm) bookmark

Pattern on page 101

Equipment in work box, pages 4–6

2½″ × 3½″ (6.4 cm × 9.0 cm) piece of sturdy green paper

Black fine-line felt-tip pen

Materials

For one 2½″ × 2⅞″ (6.4 cm × 7.3 cm) bookmark

Patterns on page 101

Equipment in work box, pages 4-6

3″ × 6″ (7.6 cm × 15.3 cm) piece of sturdy colored paper

Four metallic self-sticking stars, ½″ (1.3 cm) diameter, optional

CAR, TRUCK, TRAIN, OR PLANE BOOKMARK

Instructions

1. Trace pattern of your choice on 3″ × 6″ (7.6 cm × 15.3 cm) piece of tracing paper, but don't cut it out. Place 3″ × 6″ (7.6 cm × 15.3 cm) piece of transfer paper between tracing paper and colored paper. Hold paper layers together with tape or clips.

2. Draw on top of pattern lines. Remove pattern and transfer paper.

3. Use craft knife on protected work surface to cut out bookmark. Score and crease folding lines. Spread glue on tab. Close bookmark with glue tab placed inside. Trim edges to align, if necessary.

Watering Can

A bouquet of dried blossoms will make a perfect accent in this paper miniature of an old fashioned watering can.

Materials

For one 4⅜" tall × 5½" wide (11.2 cm × 14.0 cm) watering can

Patterns on page 102

Equipment in work box, pages 4–6

8½" × 11" (21.6 cm × 28.0 cm) piece of sturdy paper

Note: This project requires considerable skill and accuracy. Curl pieces by gently running them over edge of scissors. As you assemble unit, make generous use of masking tape to hold pieces together as they dry. However, first test masking tape on scrap of your paper.

Instructions

1. Roughly trim around photocopied patterns, leaving ⅛" (0.3 cm) margins around outlines. Pierce dots, placement lines, and folding lines.

2. Tape patterns to paper. Push pencil into holes to transfer dots and placement lines. Before cutting side piece, cut opening for spout. Cut all pieces, right through patterns. On lower curved edge of spout, score and fold line just above glue tabs; clip tabs to separate them. On nozzle flange, score and fold tabs along curved line around edge. On side piece, score and fold lines on both long edges at base of glue tabs.

3. To make spout, place glue on long center tab, overlap tab with opposite edge, and hold until dry. Fold up small glue tabs at spout base. Prepare spout so glue tabs spread outside it and are flat against work surface. Spread glue on surface of tabs facing you. Insert spout from back to front into opening in flattened side piece. Press spout glue tabs against inside of side piece.

4. When dry, curl can side-piece into cylinder form and glue at center back. Hold until dry. On lower edge, fold glue tabs toward inside. Spread glue on each tab, and place base on tabs, matching dots. Working through opening in top of can, press tabs against base with eraser end of pencil.

5. To make domed top, fold down glue tabs, lightly spread glue on each and hold together until dry. To add top to can, place glue on each folded tab along upper edge of side piece. Rest top piece on tabs, using matching dots. Align glue tab line at center back of top piece with glue tab line at center back of can.

6. To make nozzle flange, spread glue in designated area and overlap edges. When dry, fold glue tabs along curved edge toward center and spread glue on tab surfaces that face you. Place nozzle on flange, matching dot on nozzle with line formed by overlapped edges on flange. Allow to dry. Glue nozzle unit on spout opening, aligning cut edge of spout opening with placement dots at center of flange. Align straight lines formed by overlapped glue tab edges on flange and on underside of spout.

7. Glue top handle on can, aligning curved ends of handle with placement lines on side. Also align straight placement line on handle ends with top edge of can. On back handle piece, score and fold line near curved end. Spread glue on 2⅛" (5.4 cm) area of back handle piece. Align X-marked end of handle with X-marked line at center back of can. Press and allow to dry. Loop remaining portion of handle, bringing curved end down to placement line at lower edge and gluing it there.

MAY BASKET

When my sister and I were young we always celebrated the traditional May Day custom of secretly leaving a flower-filled basket on each neighbor's doorknob. We would get up very early on the first morning in May and do all our flower-picking and surprise-making before we left for school. I especially loved our bouquets of violets bordered with their own shiny heart-shaped leaves. All those pleasant backyard memories are a part of this heart-bordered basket design.

Instructions

1. Trace or photocopy patterns. If tracing, copy all folding lines and cutouts. Cut out pattern, discarding diamond-like cut outs within hearts. Use pin to pierce pattern in several places to mark folding lines.
2. Tape or clip patterns on duplex paper. Trace around edges and within cutout areas on basket. Remove patterns.
3. Using craft knife and straightedge on protected work surface, cut out basket and handle. Score folding lines running from top of basket to bottom, but do not score hearts. Crease folding lines; avoid folding hearts. Turn basket over to reverse side and flatten it. Score center of each heart and also across top of each one. Fold down hearts against outside of basket.
4. Apply glue to tab and overlap it with opposite edge. Completely flatten glued basket against work surface to get a good seal. Gently form basket shape and allow to dry. To curl heart leaves, roll them on cylindrical pencil. Insert handle ends between hearts and basket and glue in place.

Materials

For one 8½" (21.6 cm) basket (including handle)

Patterns on page 103

Equipment in work box, pages 4-6

8" × 10" (20.4 cm × 25.4 cm) piece of duplex paper

ADIRONDACK CHAIR

Firefly nights, cricket music, and sunset snapshots are some of the simple pleasures associated with Adirondack chairs. Create this classic symbol in paper and memories of summer will always be close at hand.

Materials

For one 2⅛″ × 3¼″ × 4⅛″ (5.4 cm × 8.3 cm × 10.5 cm) chair

. . . .

Photocopy of patterns on page 104

Equipment in work box, pages 4-6

5″ × 11″ (12.8 cm × 28.0 cm) piece of sturdy paper

Note: This is a challenging project.

Instructions

1. Roughly trim around photocopied pattern pieces, but don't cut precisely on outlines. Tape or clip to back of 5″ × 11″ (12.8 cm × 28.0 cm) piece of transfer paper. Tape or clip transfer surface of this unit to paper of your choice. Draw on top of all lines. Remove pattern and transfer paper. Cut out chair pieces. Refer to drawing when cutting front of armrest. Score broken lines. Alternately, tape patterns directly to paper and cut out pieces, right through patterns.

2. On largest chair piece, make folds on scored lines and swing side portions forward into position so they are perpendicular to chair back and parallel to each other. Fold down armrests parallel to your work surface. Fold down tiny glue tabs attached to armrest support pieces. Fold back each armrest support piece so it faces front and glue tab slides under armrest. Glue tab to underside of armrest and let dry.

3. On remaining smaller chair piece, make folds on scored lines. Crease line between front legs and seat portion. Fold back glue tabs along legs. Fold down glue tabs on seat edges. Place glue on center-back glue tab. Place tab on inside of folded chair, aligning folded edge of seat with dotted line on backrest. Allow to dry. Working on one side at a time, place glue on seat and leg side glue tabs and place tabs inside of folded chair, holding until dry.

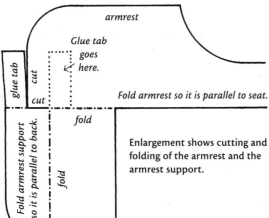

Enlargement shows cutting and folding of the armrest and the armrest support.

PICKET-FENCE GIFT TOTE

Looking somewhat like a garden patch, this Picket-Fence Gift Tote can be filled with seed packs, a little book, flower-shaped cookies, or perhaps a potted herb along with a favorite recipe for using it.

Instructions

1. Photocopy or trace pattern. Glue to acetate and cut out. Punch out holes.

2. Tape or clip pattern to one piece of white paper, trace around shape, and remove pattern. Cut out shape using craft knife on protected work surface. Unit should resemble Drawing 1. Tape or clip pattern to remaining piece of paper and trace around shape omitting entire base area below edge marked with X. Unit should resemble Drawing 2. Score and fold all broken lines, referring to pattern. Punch out holes.

3. Place glue on both long side tabs and join two units together. Place glue on top of each triangular glue tab on base. Push tabs inside tote and press them against pickets to form base. To prevent unraveling, wrap transparent tape around each end of cord and around midsection. Cut through tape at midsection to make two 12" (30.5 cm) pieces. Working from outside tote, pass one end of one cord through each hole on one side of tote. Knot ends together inside tote. Repeat with remaining cord on other side of tote. Fill with tissue or shredded paper.

Materials

For one 2½" × 3⅜" × 4½" (6.4 cm × 8.6 cm × 11.4 cm) tote

Pattern on page 105

Equipment in work box, pages 4–6

7" × 8" (17.8 cm × 20.4 cm) piece of acetate

Two 7" × 8" (17.8 cm × 20.4 cm) pieces of sturdy white paper

24" (61 cm) piece of white cord, no wider than ⅛" (0.3 cm)

Paper punch, ⅛" (0.3 cm) diameter

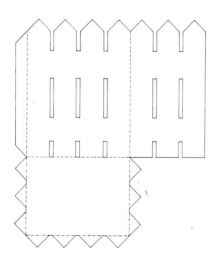

1. Cut fence unit with base.

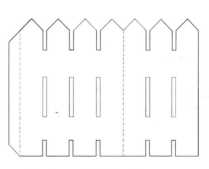

2. Cut fence unit without base.

PIE BOX

A summer slice of fresh berry pie inspired this playful little box. Lift the hinged top crust and tuck in a helping of berry candy, or dried fruit, or a promissory note for a gift of homemade pie.

Materials

For one pie slice

Pattern on page 106

Equipment in work box, pages 4–6

8½" × 11" (21.6 cm × 28.0 cm) piece of very sturdy tan paper

1¼" × 9" (3.2 cm × 23.0 cm) piece of berry-colored paper

Instructions

1. Photocopy pattern, or trace pattern pieces transferring all markings, and cut out. Use large needle to pierce patterns at location of all details such as pie vent (floral pattern on top crust), folding lines, placement lines, and matching dots.

2. Use masking tape to place all pattern pieces, except "filling," on tan paper. Draw around outside edges and transfer all pattern markings (except curved folding line on top crust piece) to right side of paper by placing pencil point in holes that mark details. Use craft knife on protected surface to cut out all pieces. On top crust piece, score straight folding lines and cut out floral motif vent. Flip top crust over, transfer curved folding line to wrong side of paper, and score it. On bottom crust, score all folding lines. On curved back crust piece, score along lower curve (just above glue tabs) and along side edges. Flip back crust piece over, transfer upper curved folding line to wrong side of paper and score it. Also cut and score one berry-colored "filling" piece.

3. To create box base, first fold bottom crust piece on all scored lines. Add glue to tab at center front (point area) and place tab inside box, holding in place until glue dries. On back crust piece, fold glue tabs along scored lines. Glue side and lower tabs of back crust piece inside box base. Fold tabs to outside along upper edge of box back. Top crust will eventually rest on these tabs. Fold "filling" on scored line and glue in place.

4. To create box lid, fold top crust straight edges down along scored lines. Apply glue to tab at center front point and place tab inside lid. Hold until dry. Also gently and slightly bend top crust along curved folding line.

5. Apply glue to tabs along upper curved edge of crust back. Place top crust lid on bottom crust base. Press glue tabs to back of top crust curved edge, holding until dry. Accordion-fold crust rim piece and glue in place along curved scored line on top crust, distributing folds evenly.

BIRDHOUSE GIFT BOX

Made with plain or patterned paper, these tiny dwellings are cute as ornaments as well as gift boxes. The presents must be lightweight and tiny but good things come in small packages.

Instructions

1. Photocopy patterns, or trace them transferring markings. Cut out patterns and heart opening. Pierce dots with pin. Also pierce folding lines in several places. Use punch to cut out small hole for perch.

2. Tape or clip house pattern on paper. Trace around shape. Use sharp pencil in holes to transfer dots and folding lines. Remove pattern. Use craft knife on protected work surface to cut out house. Note five places to clip around peaks and two places to clip on bottom flap. Use punch to make perch hole.

3. Crease along all folding lines. Glue side tab to inside edge of birdhouse. Form roof support at each peak by folding each triangular A tab to inside of house and gluing tabs together in pairs. To complete roof support, bring dot on lower part of each B tab down to meet dot on each C tab. Glue together. Short cut-edge of B tab should align with folding line of C tab as in drawing.

4. For roof, tape or clip pattern onto paper and draw around it, transferring folding line and placement lines. Cut out roof, score folding line and crease it. If you wish to add hanging loop, use pin to make hole at center top of roof. Pass both ends of string through hole, from outside to inside of roof, and knot ends together inside.

5. Open bottom of box. Place glue on all B and C tabs on top of box. Working through bottom, press tabs of house inside of roof. Allow to dry. For perch, cut ⅝″ (1.6 cm) length of toothpick, lollipop, or swab stick. Wrap with ⅝″ × 1″ (1.6 cm × 2.6 cm) piece of curled paper. Glue end of paper in place. Insert perch in hole, leaving about ⅜″ (1.0 cm) outside. Glue punched-out dot to end of perch.

6. For gift box, insert tiny lightweight present through bottom, add fine straw or Spanish moss and close bottom. For ornament, fold and glue bottom of birdhouse closed.

Materials

For one 1½″ × 2⅜″ (3.8 cm × 6.0 cm) box

Patterns on page 107

Equipment in work box, pages 4-6

6″ × 8″ (15.3 cm × 20.4 cm) piece of paper for birdhouse

3″ × 4″ (7.6 cm × 10.2 cm) piece of paper for roof

Paper punch, ⅛″ (0.3 cm) diameter

Lollipop stick or section of cotton swab stick or round toothpick

8″ (20.4 cm) length of string for handle, optional

Glue roof supports in place.

SUN CIRCLE NOTES

To brighten someone's day, send a little sunshine tucked inside a cloud covered envelope. Save the duplex paper cutouts from the accordion-folded note, and glue them onto a traditional square card to create a simple bonus note from the leftovers.

Materials

For one 4″ (10.2 cm) square note

· ·

Pattern on page 107

Equipment in work box, pages 4–6

4″ × 16″ (10.2 cm × 40.8 cm) piece of lightweight duplex paper for foldout card

4″ × 8″ (10.2 cm × 20.4 cm) piece of sturdy white paper for traditional card

Two envelopes, 4⅛″ × 5½″ (10.5 cm × 14.0 cm), or Envelope A pattern and instructions in Appendix, pages 88–90

Instructions

1. Cut four 4″ (10.2 cm) squares of tracing paper and label A, B, C, and D. Trace a different part of sun on each piece of tracing paper. On piece A trace largest circle. On piece B trace sunbeam circle. On piece C trace small circle at center. Piece D will remain as it is. Check for accuracy by aligning edges of squares and stacking them one on top of another in ABCD order. Make adjustments if necessary. Accuracy is especially important for this project.

2. Refer to Drawing 1 and tape 4 pattern squares together side by side in ABCD order. Referring to Drawing 2, accordion-fold pattern with large circle on front to again check alignment of motifs and make corrections if any are needed. Unfold pattern and cut out large circle, sunbeam circle, and small circle.

3. Tape duplex paper to protected work surface. White side of paper should be right-side up. Tape unfolded pattern unit on duplex paper. Draw within each open area and indicate folding lines between panels with pinholes. Remove pattern and carefully cut out and reserve both circles and sunbeam piece. Score folding lines that were marked with pinholes. Accordion-fold card so large circle is on front.

4. To make bonus card, score and fold sturdy white paper in half to make 4″ (10.2 cm) folded square. Center and glue reserved large circle on card. Glue reserved sunbeam piece on large circle and then add smaller circle to center of sunbeam unit.

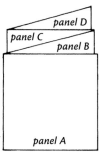

2. Accordion-fold pattern and card.

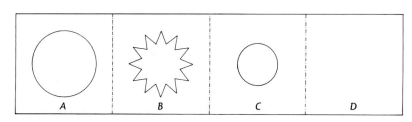

1. Tape pattern panels together.

Watermelon Invitation

Sometimes the simplest cards are the most appealing, setting just the right tone for that spur of the moment party invitation. Easy to make and a joy to receive, this invitation is just right for beach parties and summer birthdays.

Instructions

1. Use compass to draw circle patterns for this project or draw circles (and semicircles) directly on colored papers. Circle diameters are: pattern A, 6⅜" (16.2 cm), pattern B, 5⅞" (15.0 cm), pattern C, 4⅝" (11.8 cm). Cut circles B and C in half, reserving half of each size to use as semicircular patterns.
2. Mark and cut one green circle A. Score and fold circle across center and set aside.
3. Mark and cut out white semicircle B. Center and glue it in place on green card. From red paper cut one semicircle using pattern C. Center and glue in place on white area of card.
4. Use paper punch to cut out black dot seeds and glue in place randomly on red area of invitation.

Materials

For one 3¼" × 6⅜" (8.3 cm × 16.2 cm) invitation

Equipment in work box, pages 4-6

7" (17.8 cm) square of green paper

3" × 6" (7.6 cm × 15.3 cm) piece of white paper

2½" × 5" (6.4 cm × 12.8 cm) piece of red paper

Scrap of black paper

Paper punch, ¼" (0.6 cm) diameter

Envelope, 3⅝" × 6½" (9.2 cm × 16.5 cm), or Envelope D pattern and instructions in Appendix, pages 88-91

Materials

For one 3⅞" × 5" (9.8 cm × 12.8 cm) basket

Patterns on page 108

Equipment in work box, pages 4-6

7½" × 9" (19.0 cm × 23.0 cm) piece of sturdy paper

Materials

For one 26" (66 cm) section of garland with eight stars

Photocopy of pattern, page 108

Equipment in work box, pages 4-6

¾" × 11½" (2.0 cm × 29.2 cm) strip of acetate

6" × 11½" (15.3 cm × 29.2 cm) piece of sturdy art paper

STAR SPANGLED PROJECTS

Stars are great symbols of celebration in any season, but especially for dazzling days of summertime fun.

STAR BASKET

Instructions

1. Photocopy patterns, or trace them transferring all markings, and cut out.
2. Tape or clip patterns to paper, drawing two stars, side by side, as well as two handle and side units. Cut out pieces, clipping into angles around star, as indicated on pattern. On one handle and side unit cut off glue tab on edge marked "center bottom" and both small glue tabs on edge of handle portion of unit, at "center top."
3. Score and fold all broken lines, referring to pattern to determine direction of folds. Lines marked with M indicate mountain folds. Lines marked with V indicate valley folds.
4. Starting at center bottom of one star, spread glue on three adjacent tabs 1, 2, and 3. Align and press one edge of side portion of one handle and side unit in place on tabs and hold until dry. Repeat process with remaining glue tabs 1, 2, and 3 on same star joining it to reserved handle and side unit. Be sure that glue tab at center bottom is inside basket. Hold until dry. Lift tab at center bottom of basket, add glue, and hold until dry. Glue reserved star in place. Cross handles at basket top and glue together.

STAR GARLAND

Instructions

1. Glue photocopied pattern to acetate and cut it out. Use needle to pierce each lettered cutting line with hole at point where it ends at center of strip. Also pierce all folding lines in several places.
2. To make individual star units for garland, tape or clip pattern onto paper and trace around strip. Transfer all lines by placing sharp pencil point in pinholes. Label slots. Draw and cut out twelve strips, cutting slots as indicated on pattern. Score folding lines.
3. To make one star unit, hold strip with section 1 in right hand and section 5 in left hand. Slots on section 1 should be facing up; slots on section 5 should be facing down. Crease strip on folding lines.
4. Swing section 1 to left and engage slot A with slot F.
5. Swing section 4 down over section 1 and section 2, engaging slot B with slot G and slot C with slot H.

6. Swing section 5 over section 2 and section 3, engaging slot D with slot I and slot E with slot J.

7. To form final point of star, glue tab end of section 5 inside star on section 1 as in drawing. Use remaining extended tab to join this star unit to another, gluing tab under point of star next in line. If making single star or finishing end of garland, clip off extending glue tab.

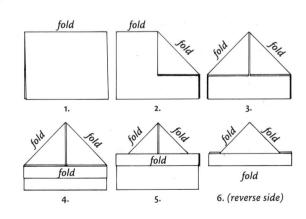

NEWSPAPER-HAT PLACE CARD

Instructions

1. There is no pattern for this project. Fold paper in half crosswise and refer to drawings to fold hat.

2. Personalize, if you wish, with letters cut from newspaper or written by hand.

3. Trim flagpole end, if necessary. Glue flag to hat. Add stars, if you wish.

Materials

For one 2¼" × 4½" (5.8 cm × 11.5 cm) hat place card

Equipment in work box, pages 4-6

4½" × 7" (11.5 cm × 17.8 cm) piece of newspaper with small print, such as classified or real estate ads or stock reports

Small paper flag from party store, approximately 1" (2.5 cm)

Self-sticking stars, ⅝" (1.6 cm) wide, optional

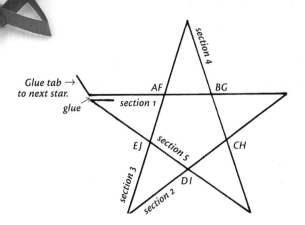

Glue tab → to next star.

glue

AF   BG

section 1

section 4

EJ   section 5   CH

DI

section 3   section 2

fold   fold

fold

1.

fold   fold

2.

fold   fold

3.

fold   fold

fold

4.

fold   fold

fold

5.

fold   fold

fold

6. (reverse side)

Leaves

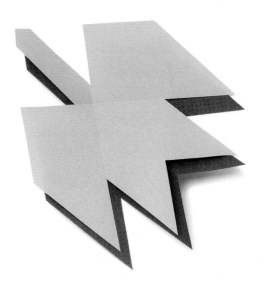

MAPLE LEAF PROJECTS

A brilliant patchwork of maple leaves blanketing my faded garden inspired this collection of paper projects. I have borrowed the classic Maple Leaf quilt pattern to make these simple gifts of note cards, place cards, and napkin rings.

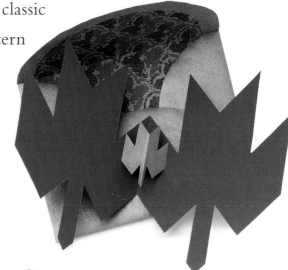

Materials

For one 4¼″ × 5½″ (10.8 cm × 14.0 cm) note card

....

Large leaf and pop-up leaf pattern on page 109

Equipment in work box, pages 4–6

6″ × 9″ (15.3 cm × 23.0 cm) piece of sturdy art paper

2″ (5.2 cm) square of kraft paper for leaf pop-up

Envelope, 4⅜″ × 5¾″ (11.2 cm × 14.6 cm), or Envelope B pattern and instructions in Appendix, pages 88–90

MAPLE LEAF NOTE CARD

Instructions

1. Photocopy large leaf pattern and tiny pop-up leaf pattern with tabs, or trace them transferring all markings, and cut out.

2. Using craft knife and straightedge on protected work surface, score and fold paper in half crosswise to make 4½″ × 6″ (11.4 cm × 15.3 cm) piece. Place large leaf pattern on paper, aligning "place on fold" edge of pattern with folded edge of paper. Trace around shape, remove pattern, and cut out leaf.

3. To make pop-up leaf for inside card, tape pattern to kraft paper scrap and trace around shape. Cut out. Score all vertical lines and make all mountain folds (tabs will be behind leaf). Place glue on tabs and position leaf inside opened card at center top with tabs concealed. When card closes, center fold of pop-up leaf should come forward. Leave card open while glue dries.

INDIVIDUAL MAPLE LEAF

Instructions

1. Photocopy pattern size of your choice, or trace it transferring all markings, and cut out.
2. Place pattern on paper and anchor with masking tape or paper clips. Trace around shape. Remove pattern and use craft knife and straightedge on protected work surface to cut out leaf.
3. Score center line on leaf front and make mountain fold. Flip leaf to reverse, flatten it, score diagonal lines as indicated on pattern, and make mountain folds on back.

Materials

For one leaf

Pattern on page 109

Equipment in work box, pages 4–6

Pieces of sturdy art paper:
small, 3″ (7.6 cm) square
medium, 4″ (10.2 cm) square
large, 5″ (12.8 cm) square

NAPKIN RING

Instructions

1. Photocopy pattern, or trace it transferring all markings, and cut out.
2. Place pattern on paper and anchor with masking tape or paper clips. Trace around shape. Remove pattern and use craft knife and straightedge on protected work surface to cut out napkin ring. Cut slots as indicated on pattern.
3. Score center line and two side lines on leaf front and make mountain folds. Flip napkin ring to reverse side, flatten it, score diagonal lines as indicated on pattern, and make mountain fold. Turn back to leaf front. Fold napkin into quarters and then into thirds. Wrap ring around napkin and interlock slots at back, placing tabs inside ring.

Materials

For one 3½″ × 4½″ (9.0 cm × 11.4 cm) napkin ring

Pattern on page 109

Equipment in work box, pages 4–6

6″ × 10″ (15.3 cm × 25.4 cm) piece of sturdy art paper

Masking tape

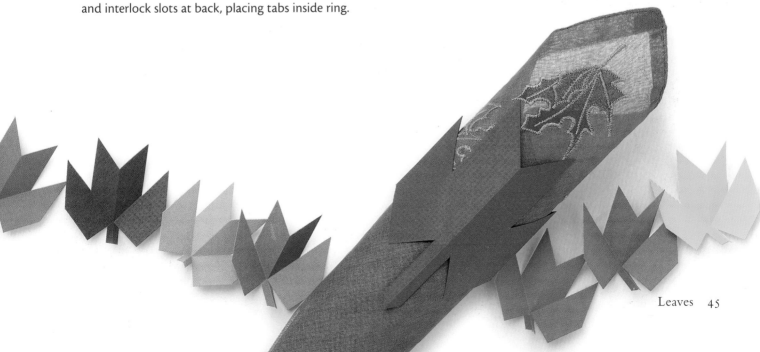

Quilter's Basket

Looking just like a pattern from a quilt-block book, this little basket holds a handful of potpourri, small cedar shapes, or a tiny mending kit. If you enlarge the pattern on a copy machine, you can use it to make a basket-shaped gift bag for a not-too-heavy present.

Materials

For one 1¼″ × 3¾″ (3.2 cm × 9.5 cm) basket

···

Pattern on page 110

Equipment in work box, pages 4–6

8½″ × 9½″ (21.6 cm × 24.2 cm) piece of sturdy paper for basket

2″ × 3″ (5.0 cm × 7.6 cm) piece of sturdy paper for bow

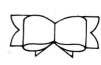

1.   **2.**

Instructions

1. Photocopy or trace basket and bow patterns with markings, and cut out. Use needle to pierce folding lines in several places.

2. Tape or clip basket pattern onto paper and draw around outside edge. Transfer markings. Remove pattern. Place paper on protected work surface and use craft knife and straightedge to lightly score folding lines. Cut out basket. On long side glue tabs, cut slots as indicated on pattern.

3. Fold basket on scored lines. Place glue on tabs and attach them inside front and back of basket in order to create basket sides. Join handles together at center top with dot of glue. Hold together with paper clip until dry.

4. Tape or clip bow pattern onto paper and draw around edge. Transfer slot positions with pinholes. Repeat to make another bow section. Cut out pieces, but do not cut slots at this time. Curve bow sections by rolling pieces around a smooth-sided pen. Cut slots. Refer to drawings to softly fold and interlock bow sections. Place glue on inside of two tabs below bow. Place bow at center top of basket, sandwiching handles between glue tabs, and hold until dry.

PATCHWORK NOTE CARDS

Richly patterned origami paper and traditional Japanese folding techniques were the inspiration for these Patchwork Note Cards. Each block is made from a single square of paper that is folded, cut at the center, and then folded a little more. Patterned origami paper isn't a must (it's rather expensive), but accuracy and a very sharp craft knife are essential, because soft origami paper tears so easily when it meets a dull blade.

To warm the heart of a friend, tuck your loving words right inside a quilt note, or better yet, tie up a bundle of these cozy comforters and send them on their way. The cards are shown in an alternate color scheme on pages 10 and 11.

Instructions

1. Select one quilt block motif (A–D) and refer to "General Directions for Folding All Blocks," as well as specific directions for folding quilt blocks A–D that follow. When completed, folded origami block should measure 2½" (6.4 cm) square. Gently erase visible pencil lines.
2. Carefully spread thin layer of glue on back of origami block and center on 4" (10.2 cm) square card front.
3. If you wish, all flaps on origami block can be glued permanently in place, but part of the charm of this project is seeing that the origami folds can be opened like the petals of a flower, and then easily returned to their proper place. Flatten the finished cards in a flower press or under heavy books.

Materials

For one note card, 4" (10.2 cm) square when folded

Equipment in work box, pages 4-6

3½" (9.0 cm) square of scrap paper for practice

3½" (9.0 cm) square of origami paper, different on each side

4" × 8" (10.2 cm × 20.4 cm) piece of sturdy paper, scored and folded to 4" (10.2 cm) square, with fold at top

Envelope, 4⅛" × 5½" (10.5 cm × 14.0 cm), or Envelope A pattern and instructions in Appendix 1, pages 88-90

Note: Origami paper must be cut to be perfectly square and folded very precisely, aligning edges and matching corners. Practice folding and labeling scrap-paper square before using good paper.

General Directions for Folding All Blocks

As you work, refer to the drawings.

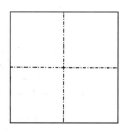

1. Fold square in half horizontally and unfold. Fold square in half vertically and unfold.

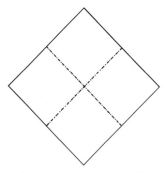

2. Place patterned (or colored) side of paper square against work surface. Rotate square so it is placed diagonally.

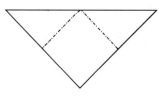

3. Make diagonal fold across square, from corner to corner.

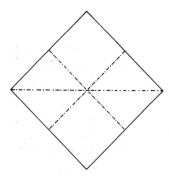

4. Unfold square.

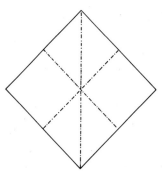

5. Rotate square so first diagonal folding line runs from top to bottom corners of paper.

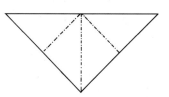

6. Fold square once again diagonally from corner to corner.

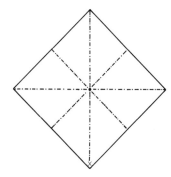

7. Unfold square and place tiny dot at exact center with pencil or pin. Mark tip of lowest corner of square with letter X. Place patterned side of paper against work surface.

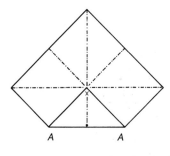

8. Bring corner tip X up to meet dot at center of square, folding paper from side to side. This is folding line AA. Label it lightly and place dot at center point on folding line AA.

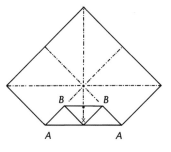

9. Fold corner tip X back down to meet center dot on folding line AA, thereby creating new folding line BB. Label folding line BB and place dot at center point on it.

Folding Quilt Block A

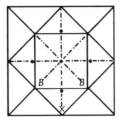 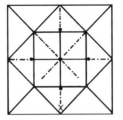 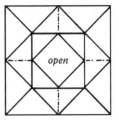

A1. Complete steps 1-9 of general directions. Leaving first section folded as it is, repeat steps 8 and 9 in order to fold all remaining sections of quilt block. Place four dots within center area of square, one next to center point of each folding line BB.

A2. Use light pencil marks to gently draw crossed lines from dot to dot, through center of square as indicated with solid lines on drawing.

A3. Using new blade in craft knife, very carefully cut crossed pencil lines in center area of square. Avoid cutting into BB folding lines. Fold back flaps to open center of square. Gently erase visible pencil lines.

Folding Quilt Block B

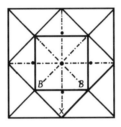 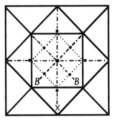 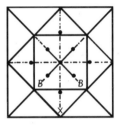

B1. Complete steps 1-9 of general directions. Leaving first section folded as it is, repeat steps 8 and 9 in order to fold remaining sections. Within center area, place dot at center point of each folding line BB.

B2. Referring to drawing, hold straightedge diagonally from center dot to center dot on each BB folding line, and place additional dot midway between them on each diagonal folding line.

B3. Use light pencil marks to gently draw diagonally crossed lines from midway dot to midway dot as indicated with solid lines on drawing.

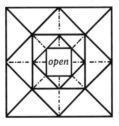

B4. Carefully cut crossed pencil lines in center area of square. Avoid cutting beyond midway dots. Fold back flaps to open center area, bringing each cut tip to meet dot at center point of each folding line BB.

Folding Quilt Block C

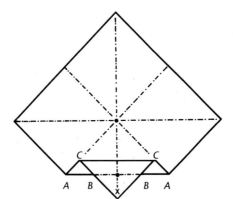

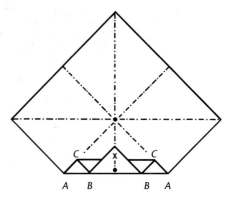

C1. Complete steps 1-9 of general directions. Lift corner tip X and bring folding line BB down to align with folding line AA, matching center point dots. This new folding line is CC. Label it.

C2. Fold up corner tip X along folding line BB.

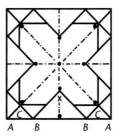

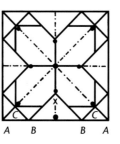

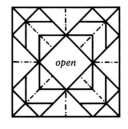

C3. To fold remaining sections of quilt block, leave first section folded as it is, and repeat steps 8 and 9 of general directions as well as steps C1-C2 above. Referring to drawing, place four dots within center area of square at each corner tip X.

C4. Use light pencil marks to gently draw crossed lines from dot to dot where indicated with solid lines on drawing.

C5. Using new blade in craft knife, carefully cut only on crossed pencil lines within center area of square. Avoid cutting X tips. Fold back flaps to open center of square. Gently erase visible pencil marks.

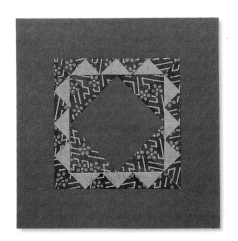

Folding Quilt Block D

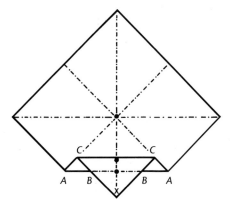

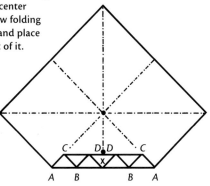

D1. Complete steps 1–9 of general directions. Lift corner tip X and bring folding line BB down to align with folding line AA, matching center point dots. This new folding line is CC. Label it and place dot at center point of it.

D2. Fold up corner tip X along folding line BB.

D3. Finally fold down corner tip X so tip touches center point dot on folding line BB. This new foldline is DD. Label it and place dot at center point on it.

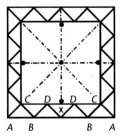

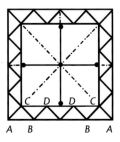

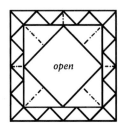

D4. To fold remaining sections of quilt block, leave first section folded as it is and repeat steps 8 and 9 of general directions as well as steps D1–D3 above. Referring to drawing, place four dots within center area of square right next to center points of each folding line DD.

D5. Use light pencil marks to gently draw crossed lines from dot to dot where indicated with solid lines on drawing.

D6. Using new blade in craft knife, carefully cut only on crossed pencil lines within center area of square. Avoid cutting into DD folding lines. Fold back flaps to open center of square.

BAT AND GHOST PINWHEELS

Four fluttery bats and a ghostly quartet chase around these two playful pinwheels, either one of which could be an appropriate treat for a true Halloween aficionado. If you have some glow-in-the-dark paper, try using it for the bat's eyes, or glue two sheets together to make the ghost pinwheel.

The spinner core of the pinwheel is inserted into the wand and permanently glued to it. Therefore, the spinner is stationary, enabling the free-floating figures of the pinwheel to spin around the core with even the slightest breeze.

The instructions might scare you away because of their length, but have no fear. They are purposely detailed and abundantly illustrated in order to help you to fly right through this project with great success!

Materials

For one 7½″ (19.0 cm) diameter pinwheel

Pattern on page 111

Equipment in work box, pages 4-6

7½″ (19.0 cm) square of dark gray, taupe, or black art paper

Two 7½″ (19.0 cm) square pieces of white erasable transfer paper

Black fine-point marker

Paper punches, ⅛″ (0.3 cm) and ¼″ (0.6 cm) circle diameters

3″ (7.6 cm) section of dowel, ⅛″ (0.3 cm) diameter or less, or lollipop stick, or thin bamboo skewer, or cotton swab (with cotton pulled off) for spinner

Three plastic straws, approximately ¼″ (0.6 cm) wide and 7¾″ (19.8 cm) long (not bendable type) for wand and props

2¼″ × 16″ (5.8 cm × 40.8 cm) piece of lightweight black paper, grain running lengthwise

Permanent black marking pen, optional

BAT PINWHEEL

Instructions

1. Photocopy pattern, or trace it transferring all markings. Do not cut out pattern, but do trim paper to 7½″ (19.0 cm) square.

2. On work surface, stack papers to make a "sandwich," aligning edges and taping papers together in this order, from bottom of stack: transfer paper, with transfer surface up; art paper; transfer paper, with transfer surface down; pattern, right-side up. Use pencil and straightedge to firmly draw on all pattern lines.

3. Remove pattern and layers of transfer paper, reserving all pieces for another use. In order to identify pinwheel front and back, gently erase all eyes on back of heads. Place bat unit on cutting surface. Cut out pinwheel, cutting diagonally between wings to separate bats, but do not cut through center.

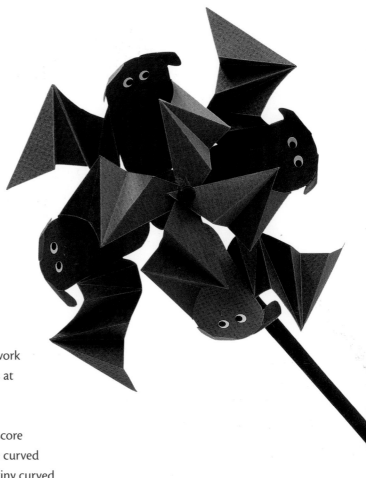

4. Refer to pattern and take careful note of every folding line marked with M, meaning "mountain fold." Folding lines on wings are not symmetrical. Working only on pinwheel front and using white pencil, place mark on each M folding line on wings. Then use craft knife and straightedge to lightly score every M folding line on front. If necessary, use eraser to gently clean lines after scoring. Still working only on pinwheel front, fold every M fold line away from you, pretending each is a little mountain. Flatten wings again.

5. Flip paper over so pinwheel back faces you. All (unfolded) remaining folding lines will be scored on pinwheel back (in order to create valley folds on pinwheel front). Working only on pinwheel back, use white pencil to place mark on every V folding line. Using craft knife and straightedge on protected work surface, lightly score each one, but do not actually make folds at this time. Also, do not score any line that has been folded previously.

6. Still working from pinwheel back and referring to Drawing 1, score straight folding line through center of each bat ear. Also score curved folding lines along head line at base of each ear and score all tiny curved glue flap lines on ears themselves. Refer to Drawing 1 again and cut each ear along each head line, but only on solid portion of each line from dot at ear center to outside edge of ear. Do not fold ears at this time. If necessary, use eraser to gently clean off all lines on bat back.

7. Flip pinwheel over to front side again. Fold each V folding line toward you pretending each is a little valley. Fold each ear at center and along head line and fold glue tab line. Use toothpick to place glue on front of each ear glue tab, and swing tab to head back, holding in place until glue dries. To make eyes, use ¼" (0.6 cm) punch to cut two white circles and ⅛" (0.3 cm) punch to cut two black circles. Use scissors to trim white circles slightly if desired. Glue in place on heads. Glue black circles in place on top of white ones, so all bats are looking in same direction.

8. If any wing or ear folds appear to be split or weakened, reinforce with discretely placed dots of glue. Use transparent tape to reinforce areas that will be punched out, placing tape at center back of pinwheel and front of each wing tip that is marked with a dot. When pinwheel is assembled, taped areas of wings will be concealed on inside. Use ⅛" (0.3 cm) punch to cut holes.

9. To make wand, push one end of one 7¾" (19.8 cm) straw inside another and adjust length to 13½" (34.3 cm). Wrap transparent tape tightly around overlap to lock straws together. Reserve third straw.

1. Score and cut bat ears.

Referring to Drawing 2, cut black paper into 7 pieces. Use 2″ × 13½″ (5.0 cm × 34.3 cm) piece to wrap 13½″ (34.3 cm) straw wand, taping paper along one long edge of straw to get started. Practice wrapping and unwrapping straw a few times to curl paper, making it easier to roll. Glue final edge to wand. Use ¼″ (0.6 cm) punch to cut two black circles. Glue one to each end of wand, covering openings.

10. To make spinner core, blacken dowel with permanent marker if you wish. Allow to dry. Attach ¼″ × 9½″ (0.6 cm × 24.2 cm) black paper strip to end of dowel with tiny piece of transparent tape. Wrap paper very tightly around end of stick to create a little paper "button." Glue final edge of paper in place. Cut one black circle with ¼″ (0.6 cm) punch and glue to end of "button." This will be spinner center front; set unit aside.

11. From remaining straw, cut one ¼″ (0.6 cm) section and one 2″ (5.0 cm) section. Using tape and glue as you did before, wrap ¼″ × 2″ (0.6 cm × 5.0 cm) strip of black paper (cut in Step 9) around ¼″ (0.6 cm) straw section and wrap 2″ (5.0 cm) square of black paper around 2″ (5.0 cm) straw section. These units will slide over core of spinner and function as props to separate pinwheel from wand and to keep center of pinwheel open.

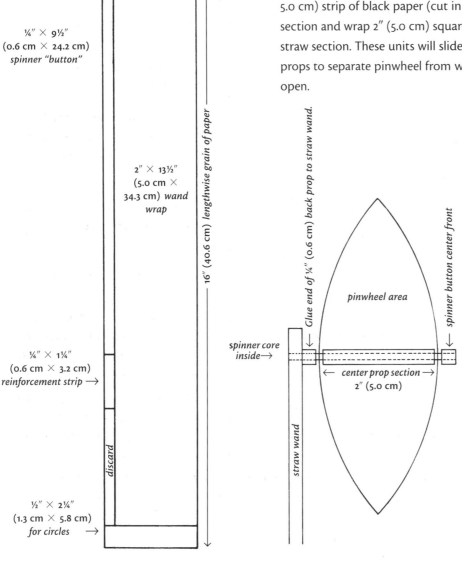

2. Cut black paper for pinwheel wand and spinner.

3. Attach pinwheel with spinner props to wand (side view).

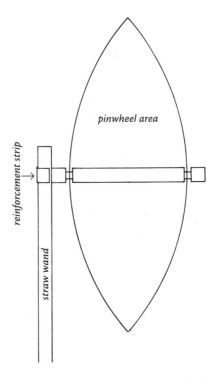

4. Add reinforcement strip to center back of spinner and wand (side view).

12. Use darning needle to make hole through wand, ½″ (1.3 cm) from one end. Use sharpened end of pencil to carefully enlarge holes so they are just big enough to accept dowel end ⅛″ (0.3 cm) wide or slightly wider.

13. Referring to Drawing 3, assemble pinwheel in following order. Place narrow end of dowel spinner through hole on one blade; then, in sequence, add remaining blades to spinner. Place 2″ (5.0 cm) prop inside pinwheel and pass spinner through it. Push spinner through hole at center back of pinwheel and then through ¼″ (0.6 cm) prop. Finally, insert narrow end of spinner into hole in wand, and glue spinner in place around holes on wand front and back. Also glue one end of ¼″ (0.6 cm) prop to wand. Leave just a tiny bit of space between props and pinwheel so there is enough play area to allow for free spinning. Let unit dry.

14. Cover one side of remaining ¼″ × 1¼″ (0.6 cm × 3.2 cm) strip of black paper with glue. Referring to Drawing 4 and working on back of pinwheel, attach one end of strip to one side of ¼″ (0.6 cm) prop, wrap snugly around back of wand, and then attach end to other side of ¼″ (0.6 cm) prop.

GHOST PINWHEEL

Instructions

1. Trace or photocopy pattern and cut out. Also cut mouth and eye slits and punch five ⅛″ (0.3 cm) holes in pattern where indicated.

2. Tape pattern to white paper. Use pencil to trace around pattern and within holes. Transfer eyes and mouth onto each ghost. Place ghost unit on cutting surface and use craft knife to cut out pinwheel. Draw eyes and mouth with fine black marker.

3. Gently pull each ghost arm over scissor blade to curl slightly. Refer to notes on pattern page for suggested arm directions. Use scissor blade on back of arm if you want arm to curl backward. For forward curl, use scissor blade on arm front.

4. In order to reinforce pinwheel areas that will be punched out, place small patch of transparent tape at center back and additional patches of tape on each of four remaining dots on pinwheel front. When pinwheel is assembled, taped areas will be concealed inside. Use ⅛″ (0.3 cm) punch to cut out holes.

5. To complete pinwheel with wand, spinner, and props, refer to steps 9–14 of Bat Pinwheel instructions.

Materials

For one 8″ (20.4 cm) diameter pinwheel

Pattern on page 112

Equipment in work box, pages 4–6

9″ (23.0 cm) square of white art paper, see Note below

Paper punches, ⅛″ (0.3 cm) and ¼″ (0.6 cm) diameter circles

Black fine-point marker

3″ (7.6 cm) section of dowel, ⅛″ (0.3 cm) diameter or less, or lollipop stick or thin bamboo skewer, or cotton swab (with cotton pulled off) for spinner

Three plastic straws, approximately ¼″ (0.6 cm) wide and 7¾″ (19.8 cm) long (not bendable type) for wands and props.

2¼″ × 16″ (5.8 cm × 40.8 cm) piece of lightweight black paper, grain running lengthwise

Permanent black marking pen, optional

Note: Traditional instructions for the ghost pinwheel follow. If you wish to do so, you can streamline this project by completely eliminating the pattern-making and drawing in steps 1 and 2. Simply photocopy the pattern directly from the book onto sturdy white paper, making as many copies as you need pinwheels. Then cut each one out, and complete the remaining instructions, starting at step 3.

GOOD WITCH

Because some of the pieces are very small, this Halloween project requires quite a bit of skill, so don't make this your first project! Good Witch's broom and trick-or-treat pumpkin are optional, of course, but the two accessories are quick to make and they do enhance her appeal.

Instructions

1. Photocopy patterns, or trace them transferring all markings. Using craft knife and straightedge on protected work surface, cut out patterns. Pierce markings with large needle.

2. Use masking tape to hold patterns in place on papers and a sharp pencil to trace around patterns. Transfer details to paper by placing pencil in needle holes on pattern.

3. From black paper cut out one witch body, one arm piece, and one hat brim. From light pink paper cut out one head, one nose, and two hands. Use paper punch to cut out two cheeks from medium pink paper. Cut out one gray hair piece, cutting fringes at intervals as indicated on pattern. From purple paper cut out one cape and one hat band. Score all pieces as indicated on patterns and fold on scored lines.

4. Create face by referring to Drawing 1 for cutting and folding mouth area. Then refer to Drawing 2 to score folding lines on nose. Glue together triangular portions of nose, but not nostrils, as in Drawing 3. Referring to Drawing 4, glue nose to folded face. Draw black eyes and glue cheeks in place.

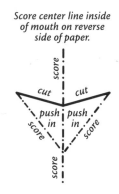

Score center line inside of mouth on reverse side of paper.

1. Cut and score mouth area.

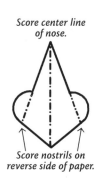

Score center line of nose.

Score nostrils on reverse side of paper.

2. Prepare nose piece.

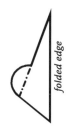

folded edge

3. Fold and glue triangular areas of nose together.

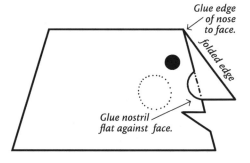

Glue edge of nose to face.

folded edge

Glue nostril flat against face.

4. Glue nose to face.

5. Form body by completely overlapping glue tab with back panel and gluing them together. Glue completed face in position on body, center front.

6. To prepare sleeve unit, refer to Drawing 5 and glue hands in place on arm piece. Fold up glue tabs and spread with glue. Fold down sleeves over tabs and hold until dry. Spread glue in designated area on body back and place sleeve unit on it.

7. Referring to Drawing 6, fold down collar and glue it to itself, but do not get any glue on hinge front or back. When collar is dry, glue hinge to back along top sleeve line. When hinge is dry, fold down collar.

8. Hair strands can be left straight, curled by wrapping around a round toothpick or skewer, scrunched, or accordion folded. Glue hair piece in place on head. Use pin to spread very thin line of glue along top of face line and hairline. Place hat brim on head. Glue hat band above brim.

9. To make broom handle, cut brown paper strip 1½" × 3½" (3.8 cm × 9.0 cm). Tape one long edge of paper to straw. Roll paper around straw and glue final edge in place holding until dry. Cut and reserve brown strip ¼" × 1⅛" (0.6 cm × 2.8 cm). Punch dot from brown paper scrap and glue to one end of straw. Cut bristle piece from kraft paper and tape to unfinished end of broomstick. Wrap tightly and tape end. Glue reserved brown paper strip around bristles.

10. To make pumpkin, refer to Jack O' Lantern project on page 61, and follow instructions for smallest size.

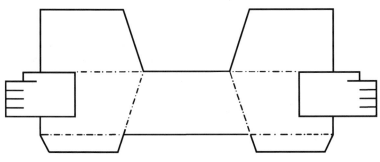

5. Glue hands inside sleeve unit.

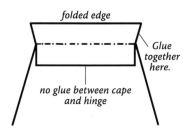

folded edge

Glue together here.

no glue between cape and hinge

6. Prepare cape collar.

Materials

For one 5" (12.8 cm) witch

Witch patterns on pages 114-115

Pumpkin patterns on page 117

Equipment in work box, pages 4-6

6" × 11" (15.3 cm × 28.0 cm) piece of sturdy black paper

2" × 3" (5.2 cm × 7.6 cm) piece of light pink paper

1" × 2" (2.5 cm × 5.2 cm) piece of medium pink paper

3½" × 4½" (9.0 cm × 11.4 cm) piece of gray paper

3" × 5" (7.6 cm × 12.8 cm) piece of purple paper

3" × 3½" (7.6 cm × 9.0 cm) piece of orange paper for pumpkin

½" × 3" (1.3 cm × 7.6 cm) piece of green paper for pumpkin

2" × 3½" (5.2 cm × 9.0 cm) piece of brown paper for broom

2" × 3½" (5.2 cm × 9.0 cm) piece of kraft paper for broom bristles

Black fine-line pen

Paper punch, ¼" (0.6 cm) diameter

Plastic drinking straw, ¼" (0.6 cm) diameter, 3½" (9.0 cm) long for broom

Materials

For one card, 3½″ × 5″ (9.0 cm × 12.8 cm) when folded

Large pattern on page 113

Equipment in work box, pages 4-6

5½″ × 8″ (14.0 cm × 20.4 cm) piece of sturdy white paper

Envelope, 4¼″ × 5⅛″ (10.8 cm × 13.0 cm), or Envelope C pattern and instructions in Appendix, pages 88-91

1. Fold cut edges to center.

2. Bring folded edges to center.

3. Unfold paper.

4. Accordion-fold paper.

GHOST GREETING CARD AND GARLAND

Scare up some fun by using this basic ghost shape to create a spirited collection of Halloween projects. Enlarge or reduce the pattern to make greetings, garlands, name tags, or posters of any size. Use glow-in-the-dark paper to add an extra measure of surprise and delight. Whatever your choice, be sure to use very lightweight paper for the garland, because you will be cutting through eight layers of it! To simplify the garland for scissor-cutting munchkins, read the suggestions in the sidebar on the next page.

GHOST GREETING CARD

Instructions

1. On folded tracing paper, trace large ghost pattern on page 113, transferring facial details. Cut out pattern and facial details. Unfold pattern to use full size.

2. Score and fold paper in half crosswise to make 4″ × 5½″ (10.2 cm × 14.0 cm) card.

3. Align straight edges of pattern with folded and bottom edges of card. Draw around shape and within facial details. Remove pattern.

4. Anchor folded card layers together with paper clips. Use craft knife on protected work surface to cut out facial details and ghost shape.

GHOST GARLAND

Instructions

1. Photocopy small ghost pattern on page 113 or trace it transferring facial details. Cut out pattern and facial details.

2. Aligning all edges, fold paper in half lengthwise and cut paper apart along fold to make two 4¼″ × 11″ (10.8 cm × 28.0 cm) pieces.

3. Set one piece aside and fold other one in half crosswise to make 4¼″ × 5½″ (10.8 cm × 14.0 cm) unit. Unfold paper. Referring to Drawing 1 (on previous page), fold same piece of paper into quarter sections by bringing both side edges to meet together at center folding line. Referring to Drawing 2, fold same paper into eight sections by bringing both folded side edges to meet together at center folding line, where cut edges already meet. Completely unfold paper again. Eight divisions in paper should resemble Drawing 3. Refold paper accordion style, alternating mountain and valley folds on existing folding lines to resemble Drawing 4. Crease all folds sharply.

4. Place straight edge of pattern (center of ghost) on totally folded edge of paper. Arm and leg side of ghost pattern should touch edge of paper that has both cut and folded edges. Draw around shape and within facial details.

5. Anchor folded paper layers together with tape or paper clips. Working on protected surface, use craft knife with new blade to cut out facial details and then cut out ghost shape. No matter how thin the paper, cutting through eight layers of it will be a challenge. For safety's sake, make two or more passes with knife instead of just one. Remove layers of paper from negative areas as you work. Repeat process using second reserved piece of paper. Join sections of garland together with tape placed behind arm and leg cut edges.

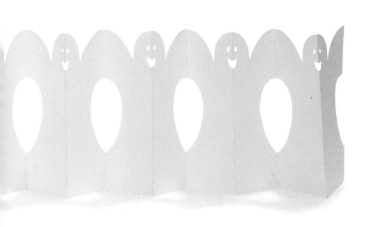

Materials

For two garland sections, each 4¼″ × 11″ (10.8 cm × 28.0 cm) when unfolded

Small pattern on page 113

Equipment in work box, pages 4–6

8½″ × 11″ (21.6 cm × 28.0 cm) lightweight white or luminous paper

Note: If paper does not fold well, it may be necessary to score it before folding.

Note: To simplify the garland for children, use the large ghost pattern on page 113 instead of the small one. Glue it to acetate, thereby reinforcing the pattern and making it easier for small hands to use. The bigger pattern will of course require more paper.

1. Cut 8½″ × 11″ (21.6 cm × 28.0 cm) piece into two 5½″ × 8½″ (14.0 cm × 21.6 cm) pieces. Trim each piece to 5½″ × 8″ (14.0 cm × 20.4 cm).

2. Fold one paper in half to make a 4″ × 5½″ (10.2 cm × 14.0 cm) piece. Unfold paper to 5½″ × 8″ (14.0 cm × 20.4 cm) format again. Then fold into quarter sections by bringing both 5½″ (14.0 cm) edges to meet together at center folding line.

3. Unfold paper to 5½″ × 8″ (14.0 cm × 20.4 cm) again. Then refold paper accordion style, alternating mountain and valley folds on existing folding lines.

4. Refer to steps 4 and 5 in Ghost Garland instructions, using scissors in place of craft knife. After cutting out ghosts, encourage children to draw funny faces on them using crayons or felt-tip pens. Alternatively, suggest scissor-cutting the mouth and using a paper punch for the eyes. Tape short sections together to make long garland.

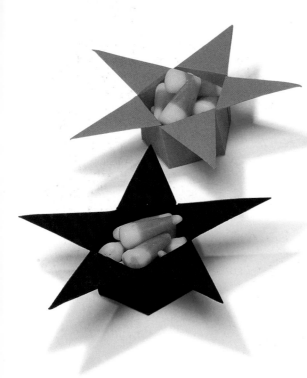

STAR CUP

Just the right size to hold a handful of candy corn or jelly beans, this folded star really shines on a party table. Due to the very simple construction, it is quick and easy fun to make a lone star, a constellation, or an entire galaxy of these little sparklers.

Instructions

1. Photocopy pattern, or trace it transferring all markings, and cut out.
2. Anchor pattern on paper with tape or clips and trace around shape. Cut out shape using craft knife and straightedge on protected work surface. Score all tabs and folding lines indicated on pattern. Sharply crease paper on all scored lines.
3. Each point of star is divided into three segments. Working on one point at a time, fold one side point segment behind center point segment. On back of remaining unfolded side point segment, add thin layer of glue. Behind center point segment, overlap unglued segment with glue-covered segment to make single reinforced point. Continue working on each point in same way to complete all five reinforced points.
4. Fold each cup-side up from pentagon base. Apply glue to each tab and press each tab in place on back of neighboring side to form cup shape.

Materials

For one 4¼″ (10.8 cm) star with 1⅛ (2.8 cm) opening

....

Pattern on page 113

Equipment in work box, pages 4–6

6½″ (16.5 cm) square of sturdy art paper

Jack O' Lantern Baskets

Brighten up a dark corner with one of these glowing pumpkin faces. There are patterns here for three different sizes, so you will find many uses for these jack o' lanterns, but they are definitely not to be used with sources of heat such as light bulbs and candles.

Instructions

1. Photocopy patterns, or trace pattern pieces transferring all markings, and cut out. Use large needle to pierce patterns along all placement lines. Cut out facial features to make template.

2. Place pumpkin pattern on orange paper and anchor with masking tape or paper clips. Trace around shape and within features. Transfer all details by placing pencil point in pierced pattern holes. Also trace and cut one green handle.

3. Using craft knife and straightedge on protected work surface, cut out pieces, scoring all folding lines where indicated on patterns. Cut out face. Fold pumpkin on all scored lines.

4. Apply glue to tabs on pumpkin sides. Fold up sides and press tabs inside pumpkin. Apply glue below dotted lines on each end of handle. Press handle to outside top edge of pumpkin, front and back.

Materials

For one small, medium, or large basket

Patterns on pages 116–117

Equipment in work box, pages 4–6

Pieces of sturdy orange art paper:
small, 3″ × 3½″ (7.6 cm × 9.0 cm)
medium, 4″ × 5″ (10.2 cm × 12.8 cm)
large, 8″ × 9½″ (20.4 cm × 24.2 cm)

Pieces of sturdy green art paper:
small, ½″ × 3″ (1.3 cm × 7.6 cm)
medium, ¾″ × 4″ (2.0 cm × 10.2 cm)
large, 1″ × 8″ (2.5 cm × 20.4 cm)

COTTAGE GIFT BOXES

Build a cozy little cottage and fill it with tiny treasures to create a seasonal gift within a gift. Customize the basic house plan by using an assortment of rich textures, such as sandpaper on the roof, corrugated cardboard for log siding, or lace paper curtains in the windows. Directions are provided for all the variations in the photographs. Contents of the house could include a dozen crocus bulbs, a few scoops of homemade potpourri, a handful of cedar sachet blocks, a little gingerbread family, or a collection of miniature cookie cutters.

General Instructions

1. Photocopy pattern, or trace pattern pieces transferring all markings, and cut out. Use large needle to pierce patterns at location of all details such as door, windows, roof slots, glue tabs, and fold lines. To create complete cottage pattern refer to drawing on page 64, aligning and taping cottage pattern sections A and B together along their common edge. For greatest accuracy, this is best to do on graph paper.

2. Use masking tape to place complete cottage pattern on cottage paper. Draw around outside edge and transfer all pattern markings except door and windows to right side (outside) of house by placing pencil point in holes that mark details. Use craft knife to cut out piece and score folding lines on outside of house. Flip over cottage and transfer markings for doors and windows onto reverse side (inside). Use craft knife to score door and window folding lines. Also cut door and windows on cutting lines and fold outward along folding lines to form shutters and open door. From same paper cut two roof support pieces and transfer folding lines. Score folding lines on right side (outside) of roof supports and then fold.

3. From 4¼" (10.8 cm) square paper cut one roof, transferring all markings except center folding line to reverse side (inside) of roof. Cut out chimney slots. Connect pencil dots to mark glue areas inside roof. Turn to outside of roof and transfer center folding line. Score folding line and fold roof. Working on one side at a time, spread glue in glue area on inside of roof. Align one roof support and hold until dry. Repeat to add other roof support to other side.

4. From smallest piece of paper cut one chimney and transfer markings. Score vertical folding lines on outside of chimney. Score horizontal base folding lines on inside of chimney. Fold chimney and glue it along vertical tab. Fold two remaining horizontal base tabs like wings. Insert tabs into roof slots and turn over roof so inside faces you. Glue tabs in place and hold until dry. From chimney scrap paper, cut ¹⁄₁₆" × 1½" (0.2 cm × 3.8 cm) strip for doorknob and very gently pull over blade of scissors to curl. Also punch out and reserve one dot. Tightly roll paper around large needle. Glue end and hold until dry. Slide paper knob off needle, apply small amount of glue to one end of knob and attach dot. Set aside.

5. Fold cottage on all folding lines. Glue all tabs (one on wall and three on base) onto adjacent walls inside cottage. Let dry. Glue door knob in place. Set roof on top, placing roof props inside cottage walls.

Materials

For one Cottage, 2¼" × 3" × 3⅝" (5.7 cm × 10.2 cm × 9.2 cm)

Patterns on page 118-119

Equipment in work box, pages 4-6

6½" × 11½" (16.5 cm × 29.2 cm) piece of graph paper, optional

6½" × 11½" (16.5 cm × 29.2 cm) piece of very sturdy paper for cottage and roof supports

4¼" (10.8 cm) square piece of paper for roof

1½" × 3" (3.8 cm × 7.6 cm) piece of paper for chimney

Paper punch, ⅛" (0.3 cm) diameter circle

COTTAGE WITH SANDPAPER ROOF

The sandpaper will destroy your craft knife blade, so don't use a brand new one. When you get to step 3 of the general instructions, first cut the chimney slots on the smooth (reverse) side of the sandpaper. Then, still working on the reverse side, trim the edges of the sandpaper to the 4" (10.2 cm) square roof size. Finally, working on the textured side of the sandpaper, score the center folding line and complete the general instructions. To make brass doorknob use 1/16" × 1½" (0.2 cm × 3.8 cm) strip of metallic paper and one punched out metallic paper dot.

COTTAGE WITH CONTRASTING SHUTTERS AND LACE CURTAINS

Use heavy duplex paper (a different color on each side) so the shutters will be in contrast to the cottage walls. To hang lace curtains in the windows, cut two 1" (2.6 cm) squares from a paper doily. Center and glue one square over each window on the inside of the house.

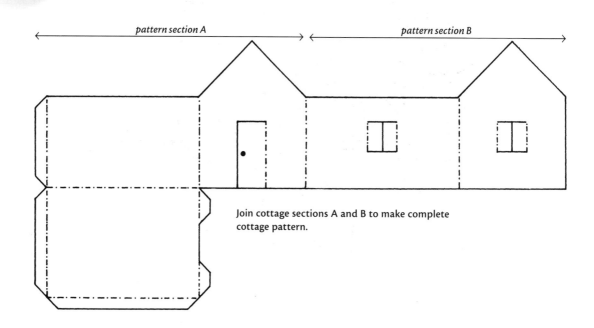

pattern section A   *pattern section B*

Join cottage sections A and B to make complete cottage pattern.

LOG CABIN GIFT BOX

Complete the cottage according to the general instructions (the one in the photo was done in green), but do not cut or score the door or windows (as directed in step 2). After completing the cottage, use the following instructions to make the corrugated log siding to glue onto the green cottage. Trace or photocopy the patterns for the corrugated pieces, cutting out the windows and door area. The siding will be cut in two separate sections so adjustments can be made easily. Tape the patterns onto two 3½" × 6½" (9.0 cm × 16.5 cm) pieces of corrugated cardboard (ridges running along length). Trace around pattern edges and within door and windows. Cut out shapes, door, and windows (knife must be very sharp). Score the folding lines. Try to remove the ridges from the glue tab areas, but if they won't budge, cut off the glue tabs completely. Remove the roof from the completed cottage. Hold the siding sections against the cottage to check for fit, especially at corners. Trim if necessary. Glue the corrugated siding pieces onto the cottage and place the roof on the house.

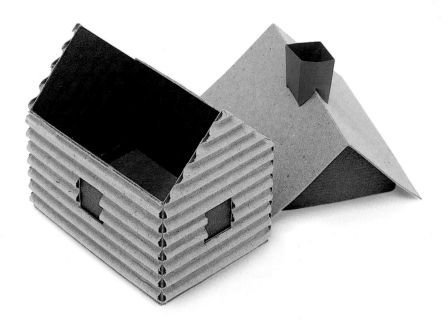

STANDING PINE TREE

One of my very favorite patchwork patterns, the pine tree quilt block, stands up and comes to life when cut and folded in paper.

Materials

For one small 2⅛″ (5.4 cm), medium 3⅛″ (8.0 cm), or large 4⅛″ (10.5 cm) tree

Patterns on page 120

Equipment in work box, pages 4-6

Sturdy green paper:
small tree, 3″ × 6″ (7.6 cm × 15.3 cm)
medium tree, 4″ × 8″ (10.2 cm × 20.4 cm)
large tree, 5½″ × 9″ (14.0 cm × 23.0 cm)

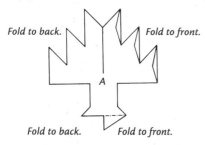

Fold to back.   *Fold to front.*

A

Fold to back.   *Fold to front.*

1. Fold tree section A.

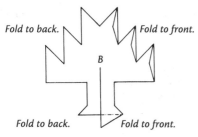

Fold to back.   *Fold to front.*

B

Fold to back.   *Fold to front.*

2. Fold tree section B.

Instructions

1. Photocopy tree and base patterns in size of your choice, or trace them transferring all markings. Cut out patterns. Use needle to pierce folding lines and cutting lines in several places.

2. Use masking tape to anchor tree A, tree B, and base patterns on green paper. Draw around each shape. Transfer folding lines and cutting lines on trees by placing pencil point in pinholes. Remove patterns. Draw folding lines and cutting lines. Cut out all pieces. Lightly score folding lines on tree pieces. Flip them over to reverse side and lightly score same lines on reverse.

3. Refer to Drawing 1 in order to fold tree section A. On left side of shape, fold back branches and portion of base. On right side of shape, fold forward branches and portion of base.

4. Refer to Drawing 2 in order to fold tree section B. On left side of shape, fold back branches and portion of base. On right side of shape, fold forward branches and portion of base.

5. Slide tree sections A and B together, interlocking slots at center. Triangular base portions of tree will meet and form square. Hold them together by gluing them to separate base piece. Also add dot or two of glue at center top of tree to help maintain form. Folded branches of tree should all be at 90°. When you look down on finished tree, all branches should be folded at same angle.

Miniature Cornucopia

Plain or golden kraft paper is the perfect choice for making this little cornucopia, the traditional harvest symbol for abundance and prosperity. Fill the cornucopia with a few flowers, sweets, or miniature fruits, such as kumquats or tiny champagne grapes resting on a bed of straw. Add small pressed leaves or make some paper ones using the smallest pattern (omitting the glue tabs) of the Maple Leaf collection.

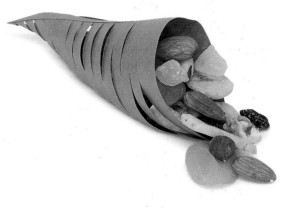

Materials

For one 2½" × 6¼" (6.4 cm × 16.0 cm) cornucopia

....

Pattern on page 119

Equipment in work box, pages 4-6

6" (15.3 cm) square of kraft paper, plain or metallic

Excelsior or shredded paper

Note: If you are using a paper that has two different surfaces, the side of the paper that you want on the outside of the cornucopia should be placed face down against your work surface. The surface that you want inside the cornucopia should be facing you. Also, if paper is very curled after coming off a roll, flatten it under heavy books before you start.

Instructions

1. Photocopy pattern, or trace it transferring all markings. Cut out pattern using craft knife and straightedge on protected work surface.
2. Use masking tape to hold pattern in place on paper. With sharp pencil, trace around outside edge. Transfer markings for slits by placing tiny needle hole at each end of every slit on pattern.
3. Remove pattern and cut slits from hole to hole. Cut out cornucopia piece. Refer to Drawing 1 and lightly score folding line along side A. Refer to Drawing 2 and fold side A toward you. "Rehearse" the paper, curling and coaxing it into a conelike shape by overlapping side A with side B as in Drawing 3.
4. Spread glue along entire edge of folded side A that faces you. This edge will go inside cornucopia. Bring edges A and B together, overlapping them so edge of B rests on folding line of A. Starting at front, press with fingertips to join glued edges. A pencil with a broken lead is a good tool to use inside the cornucopia when forming the pointed tip. When glue is dry, flatten folding line along edge B to improve shape of cornucopia. Fill with excelsior or shredded paper and add treats, flowers, or nuts and tiny fruit.

1. Score side A.   2. Fold side A.

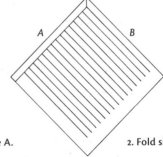

3. Overlap side A with side B.

5

Frost

SHINY STARS

Cutting, folding, and pasting are the fundamental skills required to make these faceted stars, but the addition of accuracy and attention to detail will assure the most beautiful results. This is a challenging project, so make a few extra photocopies of the pattern and practice the cutting, folding, and pasting on the copies before working on your good paper.

Materials

For one small 2¾" (7.6 cm), or one medium 3½" (9.0 cm), or one large 4½" (11.5 cm) star

Pattern on page 121

Equipment in work box, pages 4-6

5½" × 11" (14.0 cm × 28.0 cm) piece of acetate.

Piece of sturdy paper or lightweight metallic foil board:
small, 3¾" × 7" (9.5 cm × 17.8 cm)
medium, 4½" × 9" (11.4 cm × 23.0 cm)
large, 5½" × 11" (14.0 cm × 28.0 cm)

Monofilament

Instructions

1. Photocopy pattern size of your choice, or trace it transferring all markings and labels. For greatest accuracy, use photocopy. Do not cut out pattern. Spread glue on reverse side of uncut pattern and press it against acetate. Allow to dry.

2. Using craft knife and straightedge on protected work surface, cut out pattern, but do not remove paper from acetate. Use pin to pierce center of pattern and also pierce each crevice of star, where D lines meet ABC lines.

3. Use masking tape to hold pattern in place on right side of paper or foil board. With sharp pencil trace around outside edge of pattern. Use pencil or pin to mark center of pattern and each crevice of star, where D lines meet ABC lines. Also mark each point of star on pattern outline with pencil or pin. Remove pattern from work. Cut out shape. Use sharp pencil to connect all dots, duplicating all lines on pattern.

4. Cut each solid C line from dot at each crevice to dot on each point of star on outside edge of shape. Score every AB line and every D line on work, all indicated with broken lines on pattern.

5. Place shape on work surface, right-side up. Sharply crease one AB folding line, making mountain fold right across shape and through center. Flatten work and continue to crease and flatten every AB folding line across shape in same way. To form facets of star, fold every glue tab to back of work along D folding lines and gently squeeze each point of star,

emphasizing mountain folds on A folding lines and making new valley folds on B folding lines between star points. If necessary, gently push on center of star so it too is sharply creased with mountain and valley folds.

6. Flip star over so reverse side faces you. Working on one star tip at a time, spread glue on top of one glue tab. Overlap with opposite dry tab, working quickly to align edges and form perfect point. Add piece of tape to hold layers together on back and hold until dry. Proceed to next tip and repeat process until star is formed. For best results, inspect glued edges of each tip and if not perfectly closed, use pin point to add more glue. Then smooth area and hold edges together until dry.

7. Repeat all steps to make another identical star. Cut length of monofilament, form loop, and tape to wrong side of one point. Add glue to all points spreading it to edges. Press both sides of star together. Align every edge and tip before glue dries.

SNOWFLAKE PROJECTS

Cut from sturdy white or silver paper, these folded snowflakes work well as invitations or place cards for a winter party. Use the same pattern on accordion-folded lightweight paper to make a snowflake garland or cut the snowflakes apart to make individual gift tags. A snowflake ornament completes this flurry of projects.

Materials

For one 4⅛″ × 4⅜″ (10.5 cm × 11.2 cm) folded card

....

Snowflake pattern A on page 122

Equipment in work box, pages 4–6

5″ × 9″ (12.8 cm × 23.0 cm) piece of sturdy white art paper

Envelope, 4⅜″ × 5¾″ (11.2 cm × 14.6 cm), or Envelope B and instructions in Appendix, pages 88–90

Note: To make 2½″ (6.4 cm) diameter place card, use small snowflake pattern B instead of pattern A, and 3″ × 6″ (7.6 cm × 15.3 cm) piece of white paper. Ignore dots placed on pattern B.

SNOWFLAKE GREETING CARD

Instructions

1. Photocopy large snowflake pattern, or trace it, and cut out.
2. Referring to Drawing 1, make very light pencil line across center of paper. Tape snowflake on paper, aligning X-marked pattern edges with pencil line on paper, as in Drawing 2. Top of snowflake will extend above line. Draw around and within shape and remove pattern. Carefully erase portion of pencil line that passes through snowflake top.
3. To cut snowflake use craft knife and straightedge on protected work surface. Still referring to Drawing 2, very carefully cut only top twelve edges above pencil line. Cut precisely on snowflake outline in this top area, because over-cutting errors will show when card is finished and opened. Use craft knife to lightly score across paper, running knife along X-marked edges of snowflake, but lifting it at center so it doesn't run across top of snowflake (as in Drawing 2).
4. Referring to Drawing 3, fold paper on score lines. Clip or tape layers together so they won't shift. Cut out snowflake on remaining drawing lines, including little V-shaped piece on each folding line. Card will fit into envelope if folded edge of card runs parallel to short edges of envelope.

draw

2. Place pattern on line, draw snowflake, and cut edges above line. Score folding line.

3. Fold snowflake card and cut remaining edges.

1. Make pencil line midway across paper.

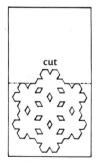

Snowflake Garland

Instructions

1. Photocopy snowflake pattern B, or trace it, and cut out.
2. Fold paper in half crosswise to 3" × 5½" (7.6 cm × 14.0 cm). Open paper and bring each short cut-edge to meet at center folding line and crease. Paper should have four equal sections divided by folding lines. Unfold paper and refold on same folding lines, making accordion (alternating mountain and valley) folds. Crease all folding lines sharply.
3. Place snowflake pattern on folded paper. Edges of pattern marked with dots should touch folded edges of paper, but there is no need to transfer dots. Ignore X marks on pattern. Tape or clip pattern to paper, draw around shape, and remove pattern.
4. Anchor folded paper layers together with tape or paper clips. Using craft knife and straightedge on protected work surface, cut out snowflake.
5. Repeat process to make additional section of garland and join them together with transparent tape.

Materials

For one 11" (28.0 cm) section of garland

Snowflake pattern B on page 122

Equipment in work box, pages 4–6

3" × 11" (7.6 cm × 28.0 cm) piece of white bond paper

Snowflake Ornament

Instructions

1. Photocopy snowflake ornament pattern C, or trace it, and cut out.
2. Tape pattern to paper, draw around and within shape. Remove pattern. Using craft knife and straightedge on protected work surface, cut out snowflake. Note: if paper isn't too heavy, two or three snowflakes can be cut at once. Tape each paper layer individually to work surface; otherwise, paper layers will shift.
3. On snowflake front, score all lines indicated with "M." Flip snowflake over to reverse side and score remaining lines indicated with "V." Flip snowflake back to right side. Crease all mountain and valley folds. Add string for hanging.

Materials

For one 2½" (6.4 cm) diameter ornament, similar to pop-up inside Little Glove Note, page 72

Snowflake ornament pattern C on page 122

Equipment in work box, page 6

3½" (9.0 cm) square of sturdy white paper

String, ribbon, or monofilament for hanging

LITTLE GLOVE NOTE

Use mitten-bright colors to make these Little Glove Notes with pop-up snowflakes inside. Soft velour paper adds a cozy texture to the little gloves, but the same color must be on both sides of the paper for the notes to look right. Sometimes velour paper is white on the reverse side, so you may need to glue two layers of it together.

Materials

For one 4″ × 5″ (10.2 cm × 12.8 cm) note card

Hand pattern on page 123

Snowflake pattern on page 123

Equipment in work box, pages 4–6

5″ × 9″ (12.8 cm × 23.0 cm) piece of sturdy colored paper

3″ (7.6 cm) square of white bond paper

Envelope, 4⅜″ × 5¾″ (11.2 cm × 14.6 cm), or Envelope B pattern and instructions in Appendix, pages 88–90

Instructions

1. Photocopy hand and snowflake patterns, or trace them, transferring all markings, and cut out. Use needle to pierce placement dots.

2. Score and fold 5″ × 9″ (12.85 cm × 23.0 cm) paper in half crosswise to make 4½″ × 5″ (11.5 cm × 12.8 cm) piece. Use masking tape to anchor hand pattern on paper, aligning "place on fold" edge of pattern with folded edge of paper. Trace around shape, remove pattern, and cut out hand. Open card and place hand pattern against each side. Transfer placement dots.

3. To make pop-up snowflake for inside card, tape pattern to white paper and trace around and within shape. Remove pattern and cut out. Note: if making multiple cards, three or four snowflakes can be cut simultaneously because bond paper is lightweight. Tape each layer of paper individually to work surface; otherwise paper layers will shift as you cut.

4. On snowflake front, score all lines indicated with M and also score tab lines. Flip snowflake over to reverse side and score remaining lines indicated with V. Flip snowflake back to right side. Crease all mountain and valley folds. Fold tabs to back of snowflake. Place glue on tabs and position snowflake on dots inside opened card. Although all folding lines have been scored, only three at top and three at bottom should be folded when card is closed. Center line of snowflake will invert at top and bottom and snowflake will move forward when card is closed.

FOLDED PINE TREE CARDS

The Pine Tree quilt block, trimmed of a few branches, is the basis of this foldout greeting. Duplex paper, a different color on each side, works best for this design, because you can save all the cutout pieces and glue them together to make a bonus card! Alternatively, the reserved square, diamond, and tree shapes can be glued to the lid of the gift box on page 20.

Materials

For two 4¼″ (10.8 cm) square cards

Pattern on page 123

Equipment in work box, pages 4–6

4¼″ × 17″ (10.8 cm × 43.2 cm) piece of lightweight duplex paper for foldout card.

4¼″ × 8½″ (10.8 cm × 21.6 cm) piece of sturdy white paper for traditional card

Two envelopes, 4⅜″ × 5¾″ (11.2 cm × 14.6 cm), or Envelope B pattern and instructions in Appendix 1, pages 88–90

Instructions

1. Cut four 4¼″ (10.8 cm) square pieces of tracing paper and label A, B, C, and D. Referring to Drawing 1, trace a different part of pine tree block on each piece of tracing paper. On piece A, trace large square frame. On piece B, trace diamond that surrounds tree. On piece C, trace tree. Piece D will remain as it is. Check for accuracy by aligning edges of squares and stacking them one on top of another in ABCD order. Make adjustments if necessary. Accuracy is especially important for this project. Refer to Drawing 2 and tape four squares together side by side in ABCD order. Accordion-fold pattern to again check alignment of motifs and make corrections if any are needed. Unfold pattern and cut out square, diamond, and tree.

2. Tape duplex paper to work surface. Color desired for tree should be right-side up. Tape pattern on paper. Draw within each opening and indicate folding lines with pinholes. Remove pattern and carefully cut out and reserve square, diamond, and tree shapes. Score folding lines marked with pinholes. Fold card so large frame is on front.

3. To make bonus card score and fold white paper in half crosswise to make 4¼″ (10.8 cm) folded card. Lightly draw diagonal pencil lines from corner to corner. Center and glue reserved square, diamond, and tree shapes on top of each other. Glue resulting piece to folded card. Each corner of square should touch diagonal pencil line. Erase lines.

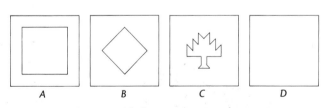

1. Trace parts of pine tree block.

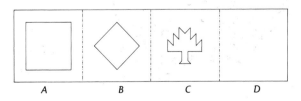

2. Tape pattern squares together.

SNOWMAN

Smaller than a snowball, this little figure can be a tree ornament, package topper, or even a finger puppet. Add a circular base and it can be used as a container too.

Materials

For one 2⅞" (7.3 cm) snowman

Pattern on page 124

Equipment in work box, pages 4–6

Cotton swab

4" × 5½" (10.2 cm × 14.0 cm) piece of sturdy white paper

3" × 6" (7.6 cm × 15.3 cm) piece of paper for hat, core, eyes, and hat brim

¾" × 6" (2.0 cm × 15.3 cm) piece of paper for scarf

1" (2.5 cm) square of paper for nose

¾" × 4" (2.0 cm × 10.2 cm) piece of paper for hatband

1" (2.5 cm) square of paper for cheeks

Round toothpick or bamboo skewer

Paper punches for ⅛" (0.3 cm) and 3⁄16" or ¼" (0.5 cm or 0.6 cm) diameter circles

Fine-line black marking pen

Note: If you wish, cut one white base circle and glue to bottom of snowman.

Instructions

1. Photocopy or trace patterns, transferring all marks, and cut out. Cut out facial features to make template for placement and pierce all placement lines. Pierce tummy area at ¼" (0.6 cm) intervals to mark cutting lines.

2. Use tape or clips to anchor body pattern on white paper and trace around shape. Use pencil or pin to transfer all placement and cutting lines. Mark folding lines A and B in pencil outside pattern edges. Remove pattern and lightly draw all placement, cutting, and folding lines. From red or pink paper punch out cheeks, and from black paper punch out eyes. Glue in place. Draw dotted black mouth with felt-tip pen.

3. Cut out body piece. Use small paper punch to make hole for nose. Cut tummy lines. On reverse side of body, score folding line A and make mountain fold. Flip piece to right side, score folding line B, and make mountain fold. Use glue stick to coax tummy area of body into rolling mode by wrapping paper around tube, from bottom to top. Coax core and head area of body into cylinder mode by wrapping it around glue stick from side to side. Spread glue on front of glue tab below folding line B. Fold up tummy area along folding line A, placing glue tab between scarf placement lines. Hold until dry. Roll body into cylinder form overlapping glue tab at center back with opposite edge of paper. Hold until dry. Use paper clip to hold edges together in head area and push cotton swab inside tummy to keep glued layers of paper in contact.

4. Cut hat and core piece and cut out circle at center for nose. Roll piece to make 2¾" (7.0 cm) cylinder but do not glue. Insert cylinder into snowman core and adjust paper so it fits snugly inside. At top and bottom add glue to side tab and hold until dry. Cut hatband and glue in place. Cut circular brim and fit it tightly around snowman below hatband, overlapping straight cut ends and gluing them together at center back. Place bits of glue below hatband and push brim against it.

5. To make nose, cut ½" × ¾" (1.3 cm × 2.0 cm) piece of paper and curl it over edge of scissors. Roll around toothpick to make cylinder ½" (1.3 cm) long and ⅛" (0.3 cm) diameter. Punch out small dot and glue to one end of cylinder. Insert opposite end into nose area and glue around it inside. Cut scarf with slots and fringes. Place around neck and interlock slots.

JOINTED SANTA CARD OR ORNAMENT

Santa stands up, bends over, sits down, and reaches out. This flexible little fellow serves as a tree ornament or a Christmas greeting or both. Use him as a gift tag to brighten a present for a child.

Instructions

1. Photocopy or trace patterns, transferring all markings. Cut out patterns and punch out ⅛″ (0.3 cm) holes where indicated on body, legs, and arms. Check for accuracy by holding patterns against each other. For instance, place mitten pattern on mitten portion of arm pattern. Make adjustments, trimming if necessary.

2. Score and fold each paper in half. Place straight edge of body pattern against folded edge of white paper and hold in place with tape or clips. Trace around shape and cut out on protected work surface. Transfer and punch out both ⅛″ (0.3 cm) holes. On folded red paper, trace one each: hat, coat, arm, and leg. Transfer and punch out ⅛″ (0.3 cm) holes. Use craft knife to cut pieces, resulting in two of each shape. On folded light pink paper, trace one face and cut out, resulting in two shapes. Use ¼″ (0.6 cm) diameter paper punch to make two medium pink cheeks. On folded green paper, trace two mittens and two boots. Cut out pieces, resulting in four of each shape.

3. On each side of folded white body, glue one hat, one coat, and one face. On each face, glue one cheek and draw one black eye. On each side of each arm, glue one mitten. On each side of each leg, glue one boot.

4. Assemble Santa, using paper fasteners to attach arms to outside of body and legs to inside. Glue ends of string inside card to make hanging loop. If you wish to use Santa only as an ornament and not a card, add glue along front profile from top of hat and down into coat area, about ¼″ (0.6 cm) above coat trim, in order to permanently close it.

Materials

For one 7⅝″ (19.4 cm) Santa

Pattern on page 125

Equipment in work box, pages 4–6

5½″ (14.0 cm) square of sturdy white or cream paper

6½″ (16.5 cm) square of sturdy red paper

5″ (12.8 cm) square of sturdy green paper

2″ (5.2 cm) square of light pink paper

2″ (5.2 cm) square of medium pink paper

4 brads, preferably ⅜″ (1.0 cm) shank

Fine-line black marker

Paper punches, ⅛″ (0.3 cm) and ¼″ (0.6 cm) diameter

Green string

Note: Because of brads, this card requires heavy-duty padded envelope for mailing purposes.

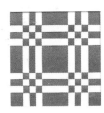

WOVEN COVERLET NOTES

Looking like swatches from a weaver's sample book, each of these note cards really is a miniature loom. First vertical cuts of varying widths are made on the card to create the warp. Then paper strips of different sizes are woven horizontally through the cuts as the weft. The results are intriguing but, as you have probably already imagined, this is a challenging project requiring great accuracy and patience.

Materials

For each 4¼″ (10.8 cm) square note

Patterns on pages 126-128

Equipment in work box, pages 4-6

4¼″ × 12¾″ (10.8 cm × 32.4 cm) piece of opaque sturdy white paper for note

6″ (15.3 cm) square of colored stationery-weight paper for weaving strips

5″ (12.8 cm) square of graph paper, eight squares per inch, for cutting weaving strips evenly

Envelope, 4⅜″ × 5¾″ (11.2 cm × 14.6 cm), or Envelope B pattern and instructions in Appendix , pages 88-90

Instructions

1. Cut two 4¼″ (10.8 cm) squares of tracing paper. Use one piece to trace pattern for panel A with square at center. Panel A is note front for all designs.

2. Look at photographs of notes and select design of your choice 1–4. On second tracing paper square trace cutting and weaving panel for design 1, 2, 3, or 4.

3. Using craft knife on protected work surface, score and accordion-fold 4¼″ × 12¾″ (10.8 cm × 32.4 cm) white paper at 4¼″ (10.8 cm) intervals to make 4¼″ (10.8 cm) square note with three panels. Unfold note and label panels A, B, and C. Refer to drawing which corresponds to design of your choice.

4. To make note front, align edges of panel A pattern with edges of panel A on unfolded note. Use pin to pierce each corner of small square at center of panel A. Remove pattern and cut out small center square.

5. Tape or clip panel B pattern of your choice to panel B of unfolded note. To check alignment of weaving area with square opening on panel A, fold panel A over panel B. It may be necessary to trim top of panel B a little in order to fold panel A over it.

6. Lift panel A off of panel B. Use pin to pierce ends of each vertical cutting line on panel B. Remove pattern and cut vertical lines on panel B from dot to dot. No cutting is necessary on panel C. It will eventually fold to back of note and be glued in place there to cover backside of weaving.

7. Tape graph paper to colored stationery paper. Cut paper as follows:
   Design 1: Cut three ¼″ × 3″ (0.6 cm × 7.6 cm) strips and two ½″ × 3″ (1.3 cm × 7.6 cm) strips
   Design 2: Cut one ¾″ × 3″ (2.0 cm × 7.6 cm) strips and four ¼″ × 3″ (0.6 cm × 7.6 cm) strips

1.

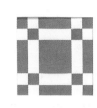

2.

3.

Design 3: Cut six ⅛″ × 3″ (0.3 cm × 7.6 cm) strips and two ¼″ × 3″ (0.6 cm × 7.6 cm) strips and one ½″ × 3″ (1.3 cm × 7.6 cm) strips

Design 4: Cut seven ¼″ × 3″ (0.6 cm × 7.6 cm) strips

8. Referring to photograph of your choice and starting from back of panel B, weave paper strips through cuts in note card. Working on back of panel, push each woven strip into alignment with its neighbor. Sometimes this can be done best by gently grasping and alternately pulling on each end of strip as you slide and "walk" it into position.

9. Align and tape ends of all strips on back of panel B. Fold panel C up behind panel B and glue it in place to conceal back of weaving.

4.

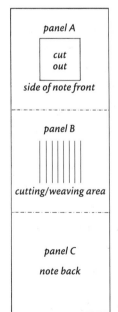

Design 1

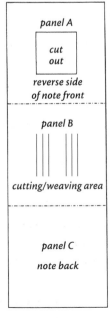

Design 2

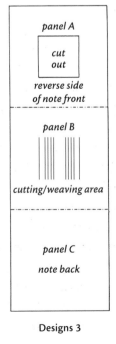

Designs 3

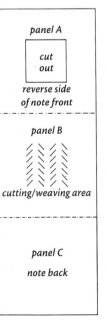

Design 4

WREATH ORNAMENTS

Here is a collection of delicate Wreath
Ornaments mixing hearts and leaves
together. Some of the designs are
traditional ones, reminiscent of
quilting patterns of the past.
Others are brand-new
combinations of these two enduring
symbols of life and love.

Materials

For one 3½″ (9.0 cm) diameter Leaf and
Berry Heart Ornament (pictured on this
page)

Pattern on page 129

Equipment in work box, pages 4-6

5″ (12.3 cm) square of acetate

5″ (12.3 cm) square of green paper

2″ (5.0 cm) of red paper

12″ (30.5 cm) length of red string

Paper punch, ⅛″ (0.3 cm) diameter

LEAF AND BERRY HEART ORNAMENT

Instructions

1. Photocopy or trace pattern. Glue to acetate. Cut out inside of heart first;
   then cut outside edge.
2. Tape pattern to reverse side of green paper. Trace around shape, inside
   and outside of heart. Remove pattern and draw complete heart outlines
   at base of leaves.
3. Place work on protected surface. Before cutting, lightly score both
   penciled heart outlines at base of leaves. On inside of ornament, cut
   around heart shape between leaves. Then cut around leaves and remove
   center negative area. On outside of ornament, cut around heart shape
   between leaves. Then cut around leaves.
4. Fold red paper into quarters and punch out berry dots. Refer to pattern
   and glue berries in place.
5. At center top of ornament, loop string around inside leaves. Tie ends of
   string in bow.

FEATHERED WREATH ORNAMENT

Instructions

1. Photocopy or trace pattern, but do not cut out. Trim paper to 4½″ (11.4 cm) square. Cut 4½″ (11.4 cm) square of transfer paper.

2. Stack papers on work surface in this order: green paper, right-side up; transfer paper, transfer surface down; pattern, right side up.

3. Use masking tape or paper clips to hold paper layers together. To transfer pattern, draw firmly on wreath outline and details within it. Remove pattern and transfer paper and save for another use.

4. Before cutting, lightly score both concentric circles at middle of wreath. Cut around and between "feathers" inside wreath only, and remove center negative area. Using craft knife on protected work surface, cut around outside edge of wreath and between "feathers." If paper is rather thick, flip wreath over to reverse side and then draw and lightly score concentric circles on that side too.

5. To add berries, use paper punch to cut twelve red circles and glue in place around wreath. To make hanging loop, pass string through "feathers" and around concentric circles and tie ends in bow. Gently lift each "feather" around wreath.

Materials

For one 3¾″ (9.5 cm) diameter Feathered Wreath Ornament (pictured directly above)

• •

Pattern on page 129

Equipment in work box, pages 4–6

4½″ (11.4 cm) square of green paper

2″ (5.0 cm) square of red paper for berries

12″ (30.5 cm) length of green string

Paper punch, ⅛″ (0.3 cm) diameter

Materials

For one 3⅜" (8.6 cm) diameter Heart
Vine Ornament (pictured on this page)

Patterns on page 130

Equipment in work box, pages 4-6

4" (10.2 cm) square of acetate, optional

4" (10.2 cm) square of sturdy green paper

3" × 4" (7.6 cm × 10.2 cm) piece of red
paper

6" (15.3 cm) length of string

Materials

For one 3½" (9.0 cm) Spinning Heart
Ornament (pictured at top of page 83)

Pattern on page 130

Equipment in work box, pages 4-6

Two 4" (10.2 cm) squares of red paper

5" (12.3 cm) square of thin cardboard

8" (20.4 cm) piece of fine string

*Note: This is a project for experienced
paper crafters. For a simpler Ring of Hearts
version of this design, see additional note
following instructions below.*

HEART VINE ORNAMENT

Instructions

1. Photocopy or trace patterns for wreath and heart,
   and glue to acetate if you wish. Cut out patterns,
   piercing a few dots along leaf score lines.

2. Tape vine pattern on green paper, trace around
   shape and use pencil to transfer score lines on
   leaves.

3. Using craft knife on protected work
   surface, cut out vine wreath. Score
   broken lines on leaves and crease. Score
   and fold red paper in half lengthwise.
   Trace four hearts on folded paper. Tape or clip
   paper edges together and cut out hearts.

4. Glue loop of string at dot on vine, glue one
   heart over it. Glue remaining hearts in place,
   front and back.

SPINNING HEART ORNAMENT
OR RING OF HEARTS ORNAMENT

Instructions

1. Photocopy or trace pattern, but do not cut out. If pattern has been
   traced, transfer X marks. If pattern has been photocopied, trim to 4"
   (10.2 cm) square.

2. Tape one red square onto cardboard. Tape another red square onto first
   one. Tape pattern on top. Starting at center and leaving all pieces in
   place, cut heart, then star surrounding it, then wreath surrounding star.
   Remove only pattern. Lightly transfer X marks onto ornament.

3. Think of ornament sections as puzzle pieces that must remain aligned
   and in order. Leaving surrounding square taped to cardboard, lift only
   top layer of ornament pieces and set aside, reassembled right-side up in
   order. Draw pencil line from center top to center bottom on ornament
   pieces remaining on cardboard. Referring to drawing at top of next page,
   tape string tautly to center line, starting with single strand at center
   bottom and making loop at center top. Bring end of string part way back
   down along center line and tape it in place.

Tape string inside Spinning Heart ornament to make hanging loop.

4. Spread glue on ornament remaining on cardboard, right over tape and string. Starting with largest one, put reserved pieces back in place on top of glue. All X-marks should face you. Allow to dry. If glue has spread, cut sections apart so one section can spin within the other, taking great care to avoid cutting string at center line (pictured at top of page).

Note: To make simpler ornament with this pattern, pictured at top of page 81, use only outside ring of hearts on single paper layer. Punch ⅛″ (0.3 cm) hole at center top of one heart. Use string to tie on hanging loop.

HOLLY HEART ORNAMENT

Instructions

1. Photocopy or trace patterns for wreath and heart. Glue to acetate and cut out. Pierce a few dots in pattern along every score line.

2. Tape wreath pattern to green paper. Trace around shape and use pencil to mark score lines. Remove pattern. Using craft knife on protected work surface, cut out shape, starting with interior negative area. Punch out hole for hanging loop. Score center lines on wreath at each heart position. Flip wreath over to reverse side and score center lines on holly. Before turning paper over, make mountain folds on holly score lines. Turn paper over, and make mountain folds on scored lines at each heart position.

3. Cut red paper in half. Stack two layers together, taping each individually to work surface. Trace four hearts and cut layered paper to make eight hearts. Score and mountain-fold center line on each heart and glue in place on wreath, front or back, depending on look you prefer. If desired, cut hearts for both sides of wreath. To make hanging loop, pass end of string through hole and tie ends in bow.

Materials

For one 4¼″ (10.8 cm) diameter Holly Heart Ornament (pictured directly above)

....

Patterns on page 129

Equipment in work box, pages 4–6

5″ (12.8 cm) square of acetate

5″ (12.8 cm) square of sturdy green paper

4″ (10.2 cm) square of stationery-weight red paper

12″ (30.5 cm) length of red string

Paper punch, ⅛″ (0.3 cm) diameter

SANTA SLEIGH

Trim your tree or tabletop with one of these Santa Sleighs. For cargo, add a ribbon-tied bag of treats, a small teddy cozied within a tartan blanket, a stack of miniature gift-wrapped Christmas packages, or all of the above.

Materials

For one small or one large sleigh

Patterns on pages 131–132

Equipment in work box, pages 4-6

Piece of red paper:
small, 4¼" × 5¼" (10.8 cm × 13.4 cm)
large, 7" × 8½" (17.8 cm × 21.6 cm)

Piece of green paper:
small, 3¼" × 5¼" (8.3 cm × 13.4 cm)
large, 5¼" × 8½" (13.4 cm × 21.6 cm)

Instructions

1. Photocopy small or large patterns for sled and runner, or trace patterns transferring all markings. Cut out patterns including small design areas within runners. Pierce patterns with pin to indicate folding lines.

2. Use tape or clips to anchor patterns on paper and use pencil to draw round outside shapes and inside runners. Push pencil into pinholes indicating folding lines. Remove patterns. Finish drawing all lines marked with pencil dots.

3. Cut out sled with craft knife on protected surface. Score and crease on folding lines and glue ends to sides. Before cutting runner section, cut out small design areas within it. Score and crease folding lines, but do not add glue at this time.

4. Spread thin layer of glue on bottom of sled and place it on platform area of flattened runner piece, aligning back corner of sled with back edge of runner. When dry, refold runner and glue tab in place.

STAR CHAIN

The star motif, a symbol of faith for both the Christian and Jewish religious traditions, inspired these decorative garlands for Christmas and Hanukkah celebrations. The leftover shapes cut from the center of each star link can be used as place cards or gift tags for these two festive occasions. See page 130 for Star of David pattern.

Instructions

1. Photocopy pattern of your choice from page 130, or trace it, but do not cut out. Spread glue on reverse side of uncut pattern and press it against acetate. Allow to dry.

2. Using craft knife and straightedge on protected work surface, cut out pattern for star. Also cut out star at center, leaving only ¼" (0.6 cm) outline of shape for pattern.

3. Tape or clip pattern to paper and draw around and within star shape. Remove pattern. Depending on thickness of paper it might be possible to cut 2 or 3 links at once. Be sure to tape papers together so they won't shift when cut. Carefully cut out star and smaller star within it, reserving smaller one for place cards or gift bags. To open each large star link, make cut as indicated on pattern. Intertwine stars to make chain of any length. To close star links, use pin to spread very thin layer of glue right on clipped edges. Then align cut edges and don't move paper until dry. If this method doesn't work well on your paper, punch ¼" (0.6 cm) dot from matching paper scraps and glue it like a Band-Aid over cut edges.

Materials

For each link of chain

Pattern on page 130

Equipment in work box, pages 4–6

4¾" (12.0 cm) square of acetate

4¾" (12.0 cm) square of sturdy paper

Paper punch, ¼" (0.6 cm) diameter circle

Appendix
& Patterns

APPENDIX

Making Envelopes

Several standard sizes of envelopes can be purchased affordably and in quantity at discount stores, office suppliers, and supermarkets, but color and quality choices are usually rather limited at these outlets. Craft stores frequently offer a greater selection, but the price is usually greater too, so why not try making your own envelopes? It is fun and truly a quick and easy task once you have made the patterns, and the choices of color, texture, and size will be unlimited. In order to be acceptable for mailing, however, envelopes must conform to certain postal standards regarding minimum size, proper height-to-length ratio, and maximum thickness of contents. To avoid postal surcharges as well as delivery delays due to returned unacceptable envelopes, visit your post office and request information about current standards or ask for a photocopy of the template that clerks use to check mail dimensions. At the time of writing, all the envelopes in this book meet the United States Postal Service requirements.

General Directions for All Envelopes

Instructions

Materials

For one envelope A, B, C, or D

Pattern size of your choice, pages 90–91

Equipment in work box, pages 4-6

Paper of your choice (size requirements on pattern)

1. Select envelope size of your choice—A, B, C, or D. Dimensions are indicated on patterns. Refer to Drawing 1 and trace rectangular envelope shape. Also make two tracings of semicircular top and bottom flap and two tracings of semicircular side flap. For greatest accuracy, use compass to trace semicircles. Cut out all pattern pieces. Referring to Drawing 2, arrange envelope pieces in proper order on work surface and tape them together. Practice folding envelope pattern to check for alignment of flaps. Referring to Drawing 3, trace pattern for optional liner circle on folded paper and cut it out. If you wish to extend life of patterns, glue them to acetate.

2. Referring to Drawing 4A or 4B, place paper of your choice right-side up on protected work surface. Tape or clip pattern onto paper and draw around pattern shape. Remove pattern. Still referring to Drawing 4A or 4B, draw and score perpendicular lines within outlined shape to define straight edges of envelope. Cut out shape and flip it over to reverse side of paper.

3. Referring to Drawing 5, fold in side flaps. Apply glue to edges of bottom flap, avoiding center area.

4. Referring to Drawing 6, fold up bottom flap so it overlaps side flaps. To protect interior of envelope from misplaced glue, slide in a piece of scrap paper to keep front and back layers separated. Allow glue to dry. Remove scrap paper.

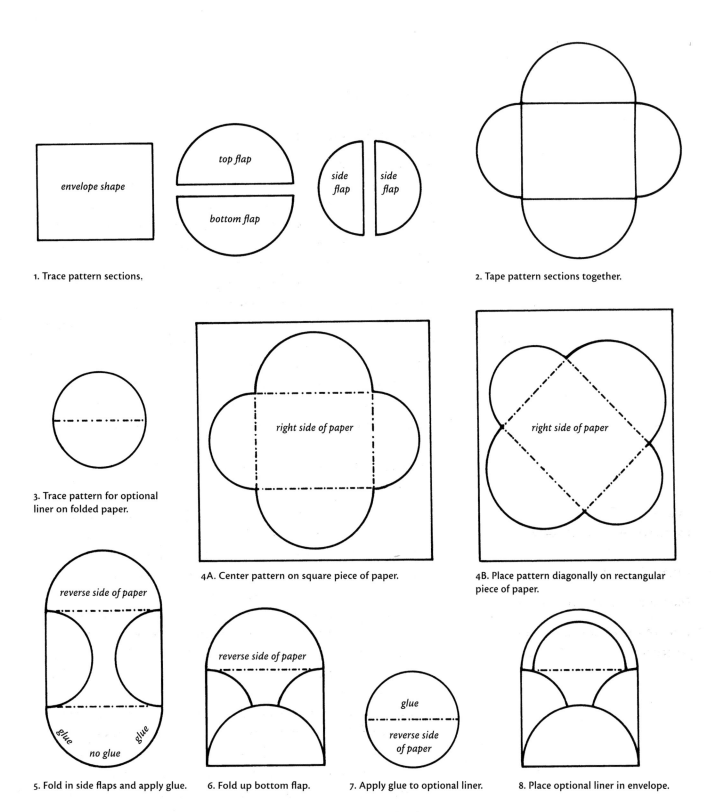

1. Trace pattern sections.

2. Tape pattern sections together.

3. Trace pattern for optional liner on folded paper.

4A. Center pattern on square piece of paper.

4B. Place pattern diagonally on rectangular piece of paper.

5. Fold in side flaps and apply glue.

6. Fold up bottom flap.

7. Apply glue to optional liner.

8. Place optional liner in envelope.

envelope shape

top flap

bottom flap

side flap *side flap*

right side of paper

right side of paper

reverse side of paper

reverse side of paper

glue

reverse side of paper

glue glue

no glue

5. If you wish to add liner, refer to Drawing 7. Flip liner over to reverse side and apply glue to only half of circle above folding line. Slide unglued portion of liner inside envelope, as in Drawing 8. Center glued portion of liner on top flap, aligning folds, and press two layers together. Immediately fold down top flap to finalize placement of liner. In order to hinge well, folding lines of liner and envelope will probably shift and not be aligned after folding down top flap. Insert card and seal envelope.

Envelopes

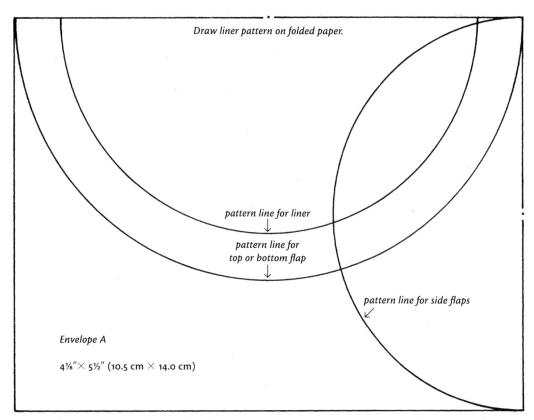

Draw liner pattern on folded paper.

pattern line for liner

*pattern line for
top or bottom flap*

pattern line for side flaps

Envelope A

4⅛″ × 5½″ (10.5 cm × 14.0 cm)

Envelope A: Refer to general directions for all envelopes and center complete pattern on 10″ (25.4 cm) square of paper or place diagonally on 8½″ × 11″ (21.6 cm × 28 cm) piece of paper.

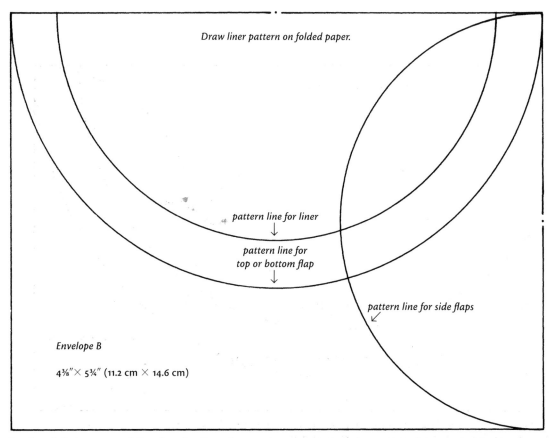

Draw liner pattern on folded paper.

pattern line for liner

*pattern line for
top or bottom flap*

pattern line for side flaps

Envelope B

4⅜″ × 5¾″ (11.2 cm × 14.6 cm)

Envelope B: Refer to general directions for all envelopes and center complete pattern on 10½″ (26.6 cm) square of paper or place diagonally on 9″ × 12″ (22.8 cm × 30.5 cm) piece of paper.

Envelopes

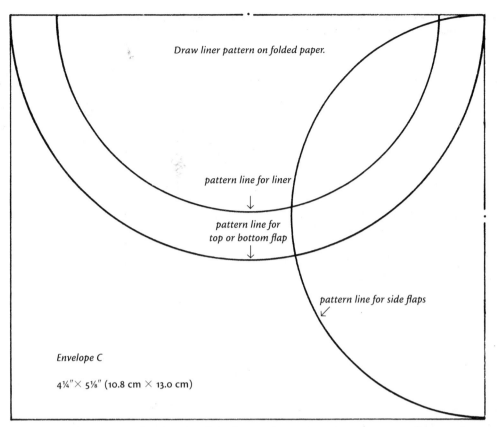

Draw liner pattern on folded paper.

pattern line for liner
↓

*pattern line for
top or bottom flap*
↓

pattern line for side flaps
↙

Envelope C

4¼″ × 5⅛″ (10.8 cm × 13.0 cm)

Envelope C: Refer to general directions for all envelopes and center complete pattern on 9¾″ (24.8 cm) square of paper or place diagonally on 8½″ × 11″ (21.6 cm × 28.0 cm) piece of paper.

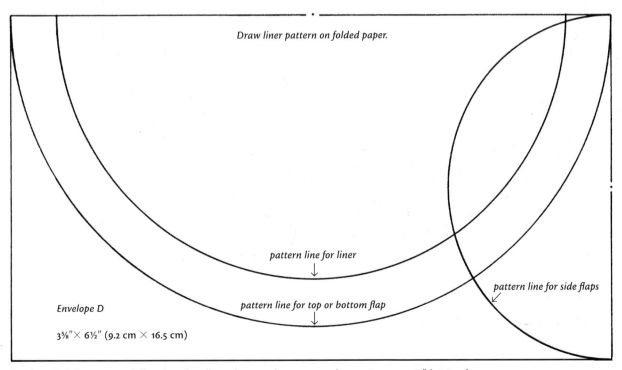

Draw liner pattern on folded paper.

pattern line for liner
↓

pattern line for top or bottom flap
↓

pattern line for side flaps
↙

Envelope D

3⅝″ × 6½″ (9.2 cm × 16.5 cm)

Envelope D: Refer to general directions for all envelopes and center complete pattern on 10½″ (26.6 cm) square of paper or place diagonally on 9″ × 12″ (22.8 cm × 30.5 cm) piece of paper.

Petal Bowls

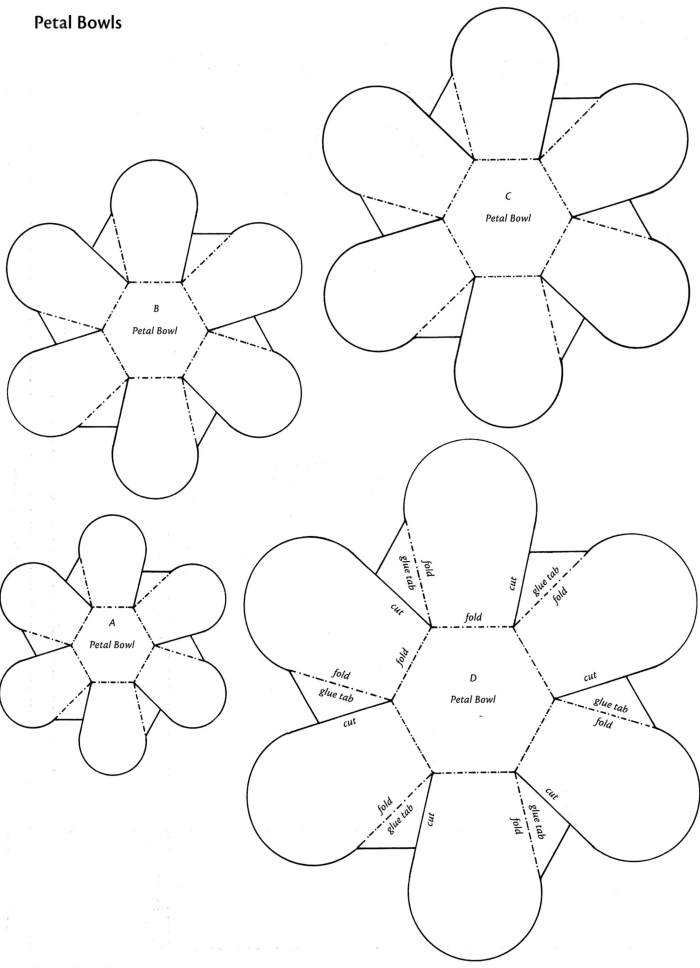

B
Petal Bowl

C
Petal Bowl

A
Petal Bowl

D
Petal Bowl

fold
glue tab
cut
cut
glue tab
fold
fold
fold
fold
glue tab
cut
cut
glue tab
fold
fold
glue tab
cut
cut
glue tab
fold

Feathered Hearts

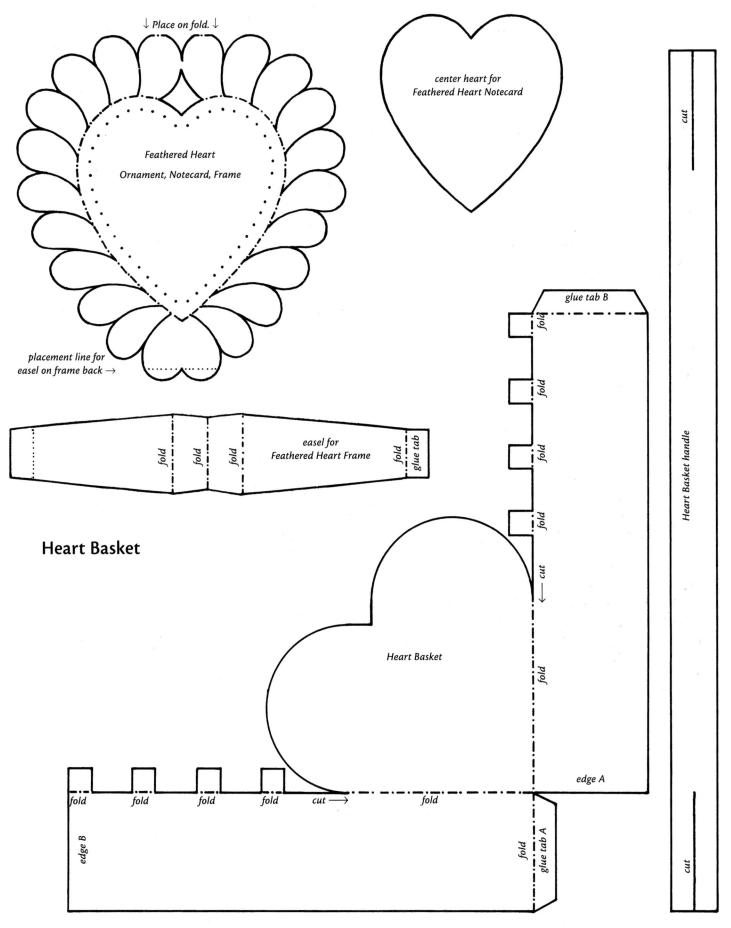

↓ *Place on fold.* ↓

Feathered Heart
Ornament, Notecard, Frame

center heart for
Feathered Heart Notecard

placement line for
easel on frame back →

fold   fold   fold   *easel for*
Feathered Heart Frame   fold   glue tab

Heart Basket

glue tab B

fold

fold

fold

fold

← cut

fold

Heart Basket handle

Heart Basket

edge A

fold   fold   fold   fold   cut →   fold

edge B

fold   glue tab A

cut

cut

Quilt-Block Valentine

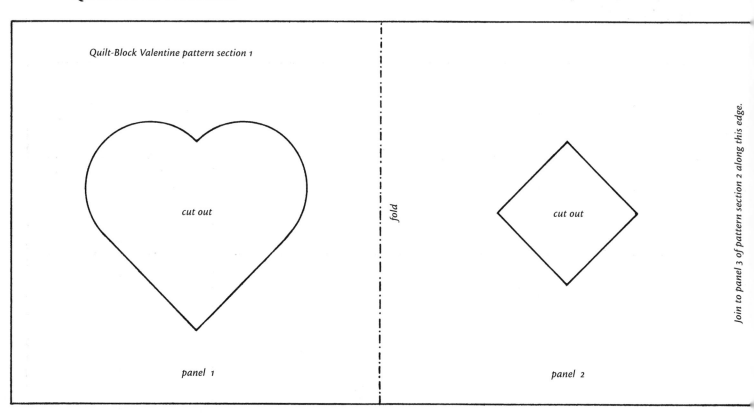

Quilt-Block Valentine pattern section 1

cut out

fold

cut out

Join to panel 3 of pattern section 2 along this edge.

panel 1

panel 2

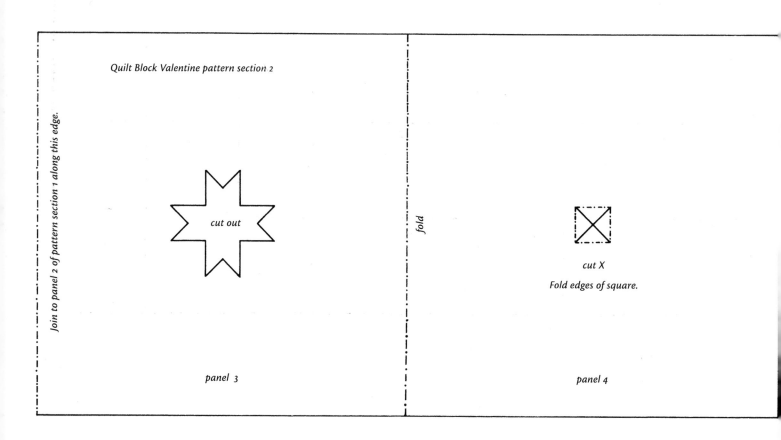

Quilt Block Valentine pattern section 2

cut out

Join to panel 2 of pattern section 1 along this edge.

fold

cut X

Fold edges of square.

panel 3

panel 4

cut D

fold A1

← fold A3

← fold D3

fold A2

cut A

fold D1

fold D2

fold B2

fold B1

No-Glue Gift Box
small box lid

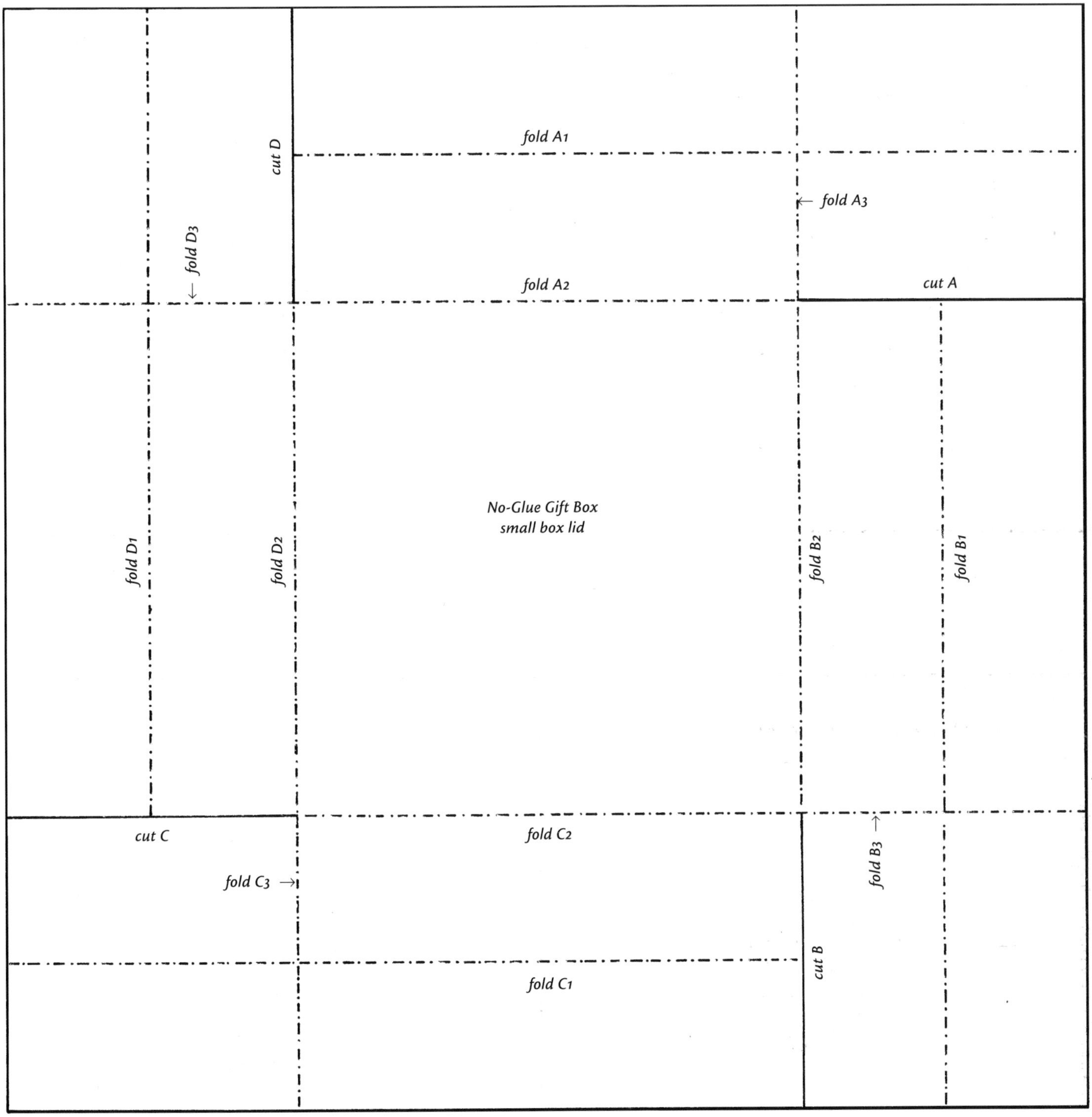

cut C

fold C2

fold C3 →

fold B3 →

cut B

fold C1

No-Glue Gift Box
small box base

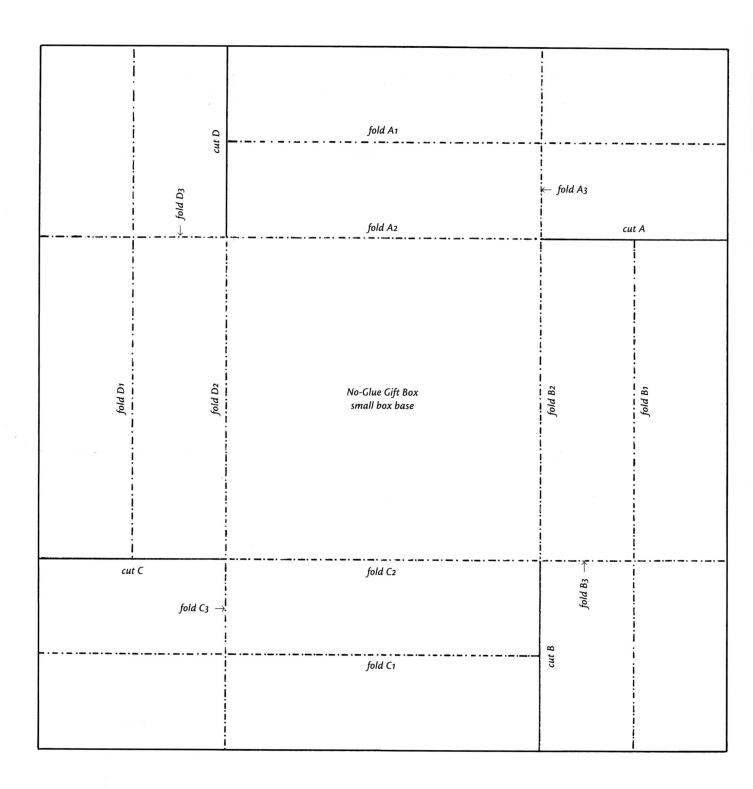

Baby Shirt Card

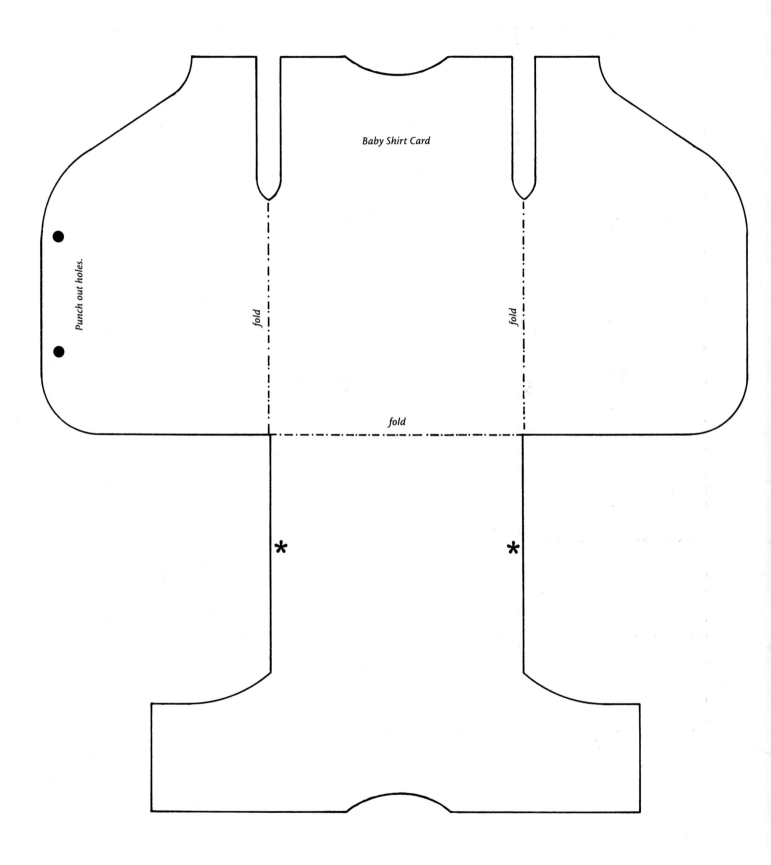

Baby Shirt Card

Punch out holes.

fold

fold

fold

*

*

Baby Shoe Baskets

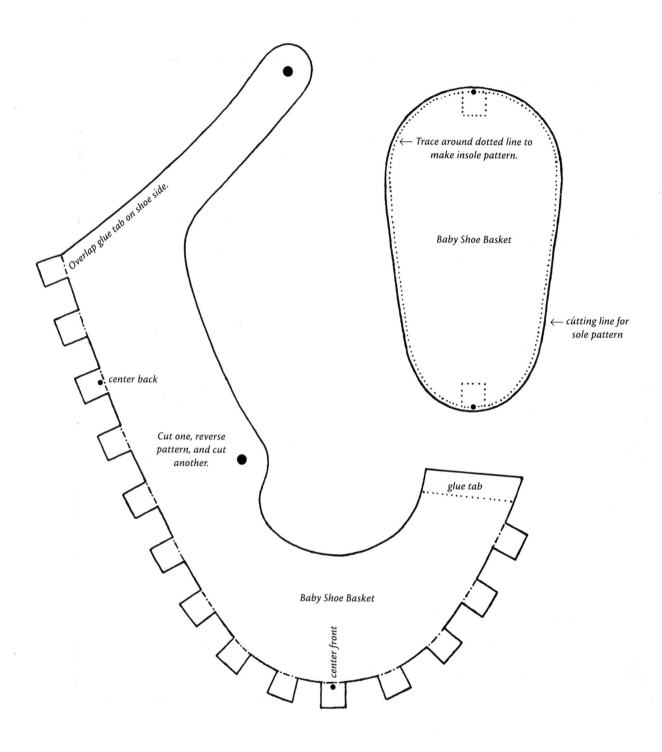

Overlap glue tab on shoe side.

• center back

Cut one, reverse pattern, and cut another.

Baby Shoe Basket

center front

← Trace around dotted line to make insole pattern.

Baby Shoe Basket

← cutting line for sole pattern

glue tab

Photograph Portfolio

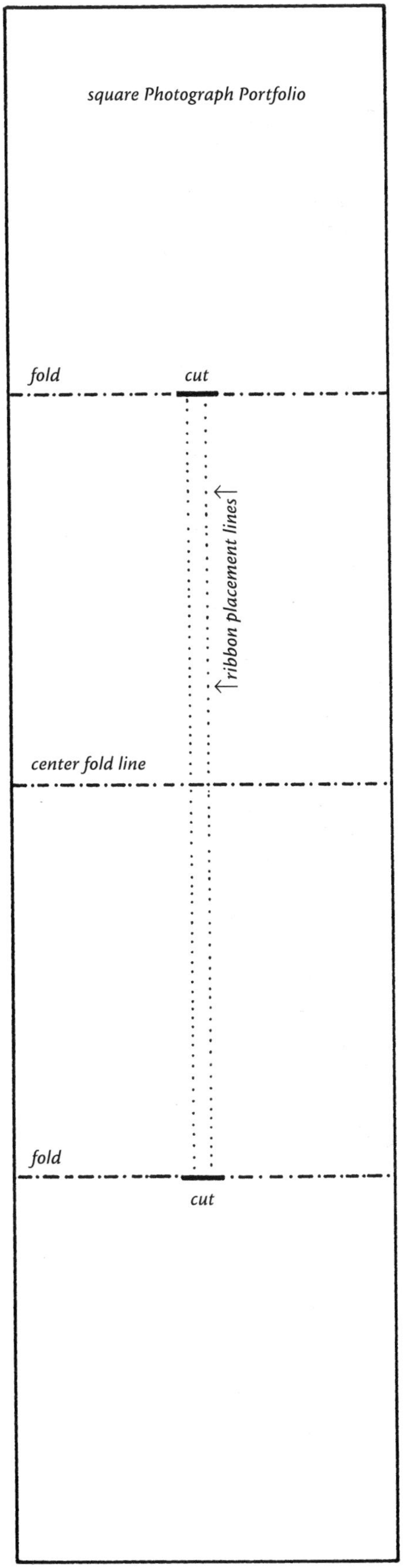

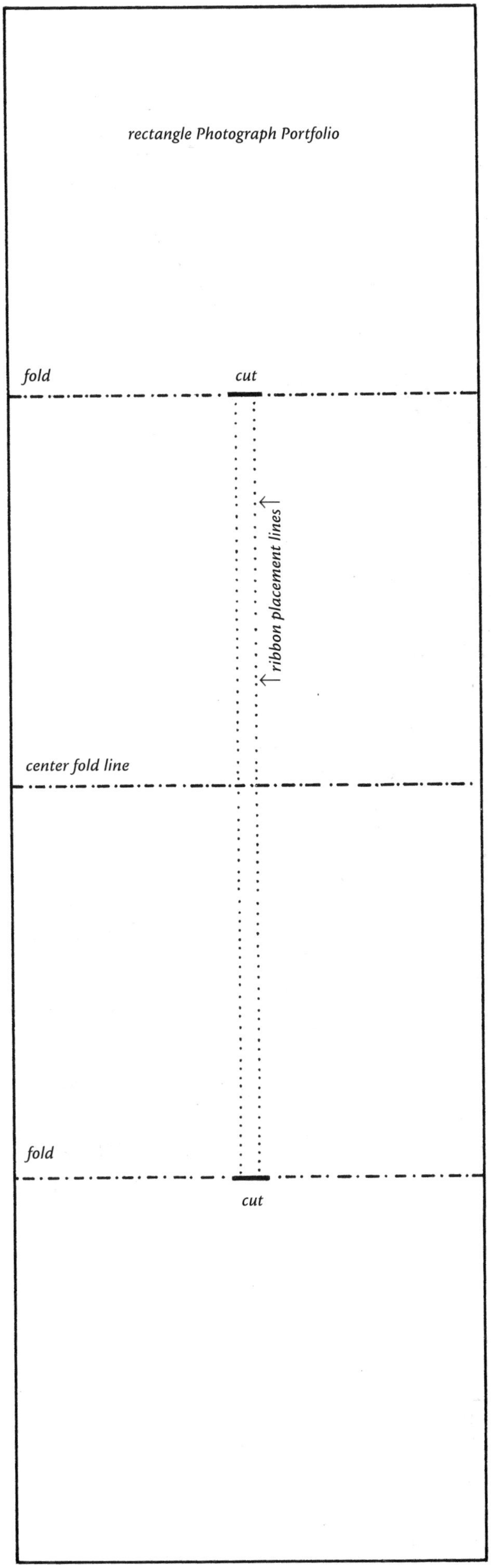

square Photograph Portfolio

fold   cut

↑ ribbon placement lines ↑

center fold line

fold
                        cut

rectangle Photograph Portfolio

fold   cut

↑ ribbon placement lines ↑

center fold line

fold
                        cut

Lace Easter Egg Card

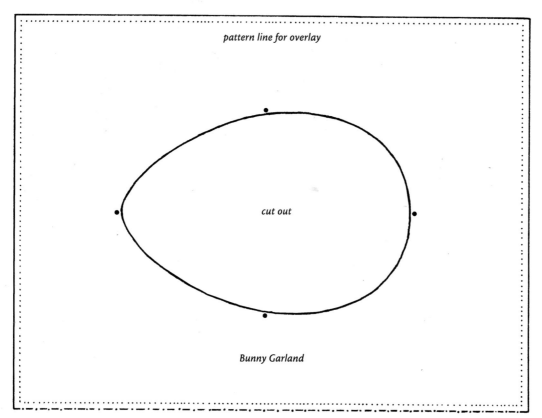

pattern line for overlay

cut out

Bunny Garland

Place on fold.

Bunny Note and Garland

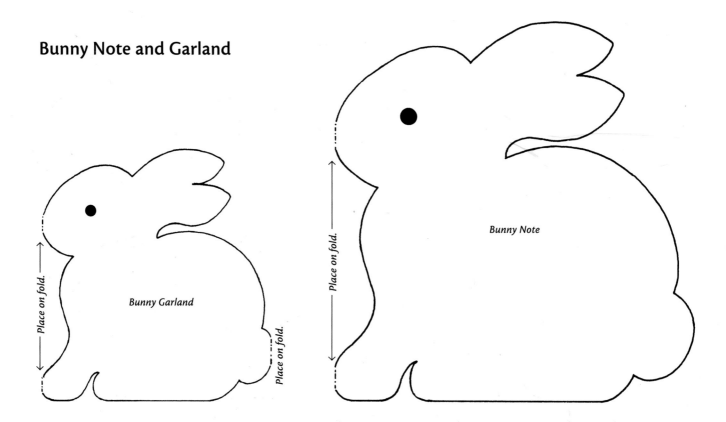

Bunny Garland

Place on fold.

Place on fold.

Place on fold.

Bunny Note

Page Corner Bookmarks

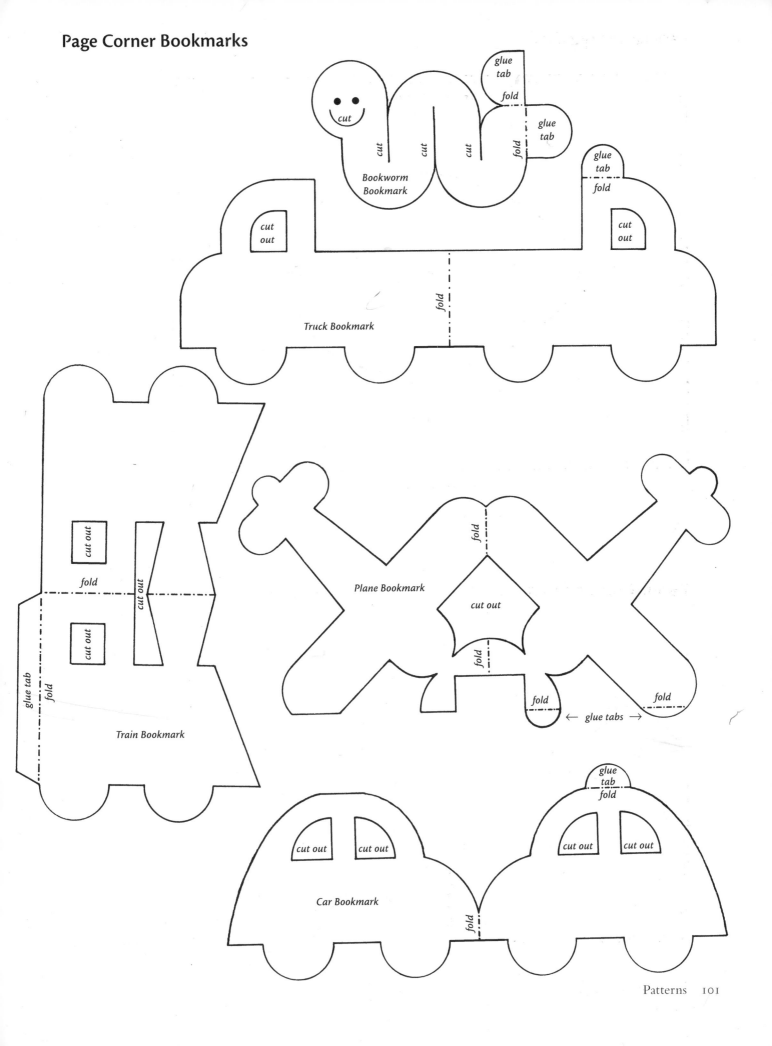

Bookworm Bookmark

Truck Bookmark

Train Bookmark

Plane Bookmark

Car Bookmark

Watering Can

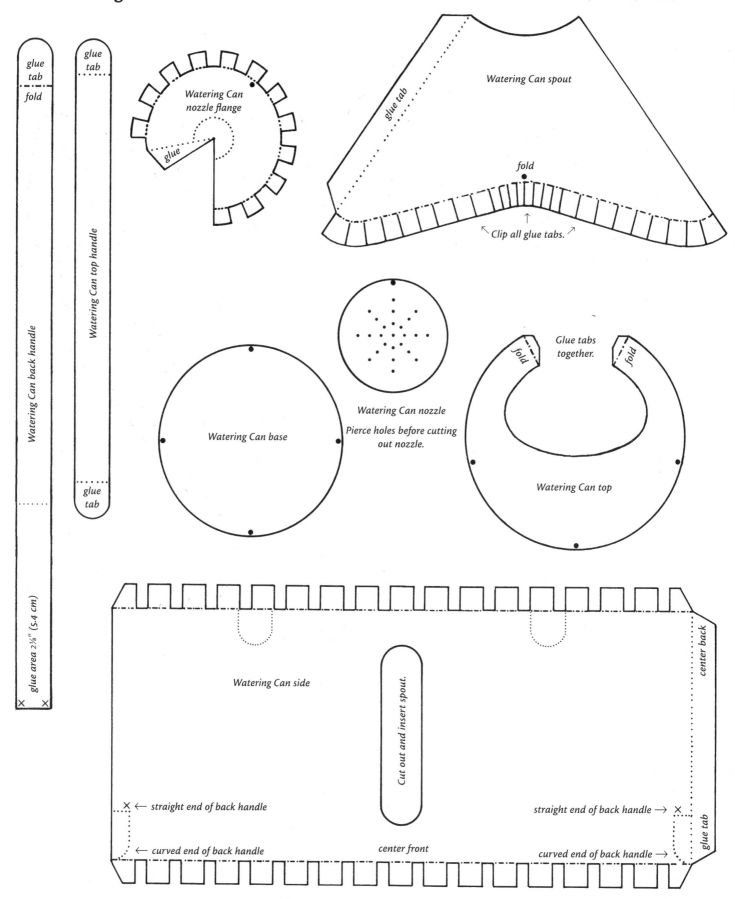

glue tab

glue tab

fold

Watering Can nozzle flange

glue

Watering Can spout

glue tab

fold

← Clip all glue tabs. →

Watering Can back handle

Watering Can top handle

glue tab

Watering Can base

Watering Can nozzle

Pierce holes before cutting out nozzle.

Glue tabs together.

fold

fold

Watering Can top

glue area 2⅛″ (5.4 cm)

✕ ✕

Watering Can side

Cut out and insert spout.

center back

✕ ← straight end of back handle

straight end of back handle → ✕

← curved end of back handle

center front

curved end of back handle →

glue tab

May Basket

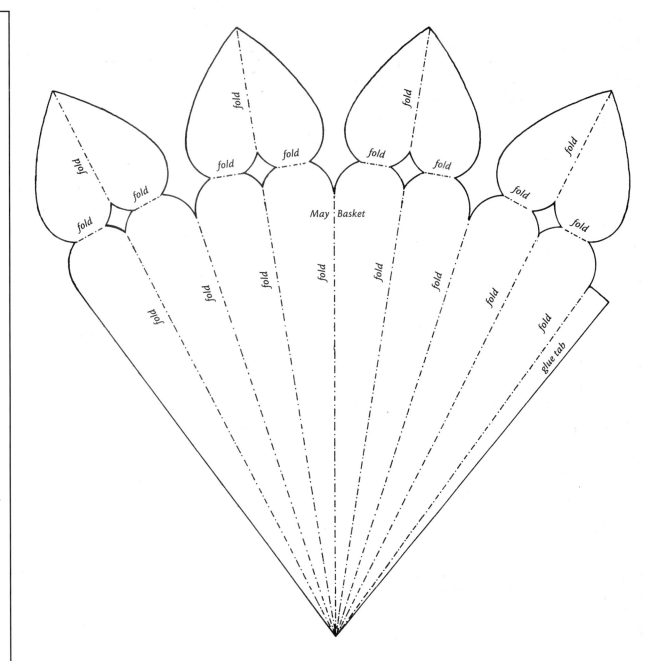

May Basket handle

fold fold fold fold fold fold

fold fold fold fold

May Basket

fold fold fold fold fold fold fold fold

glue tab

Adirondack Chair

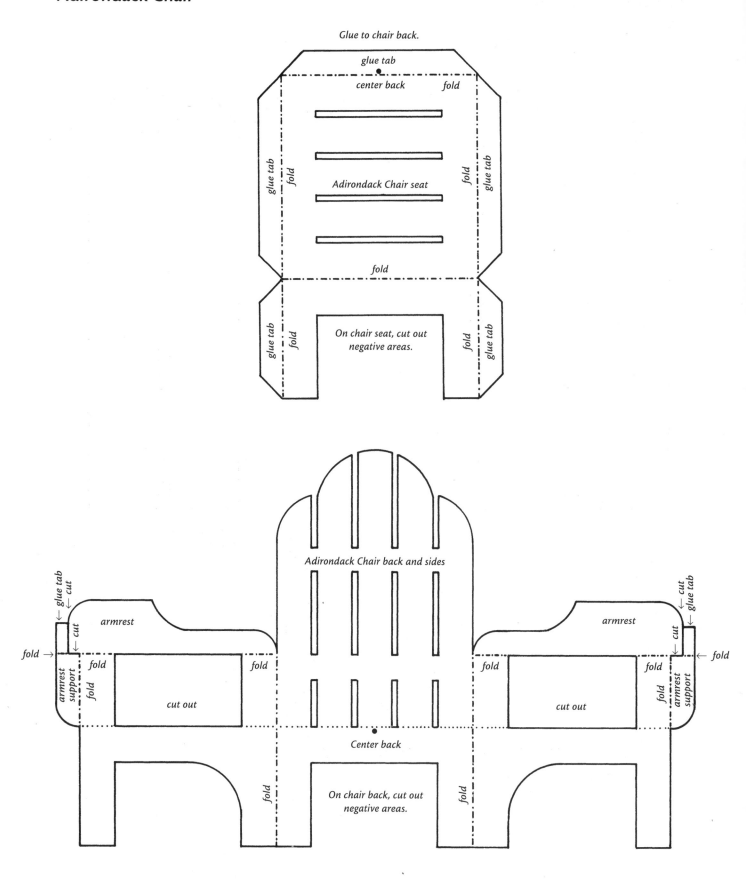

Glue to chair back.

glue tab

center back   fold

glue tab

fold

glue tab fold

Adirondack Chair seat

fold glue tab

fold

glue tab fold

On chair seat, cut out negative areas.

fold glue tab

glue tab cut

cut

armrest

Adirondack Chair back and sides

armrest

cut glue tab

cut

fold →

armrest support fold fold

cut out

fold

fold fold armrest support

← fold

cut out

fold

Center back

On chair back, cut out negative areas.

Picket-Fence Gift Tote

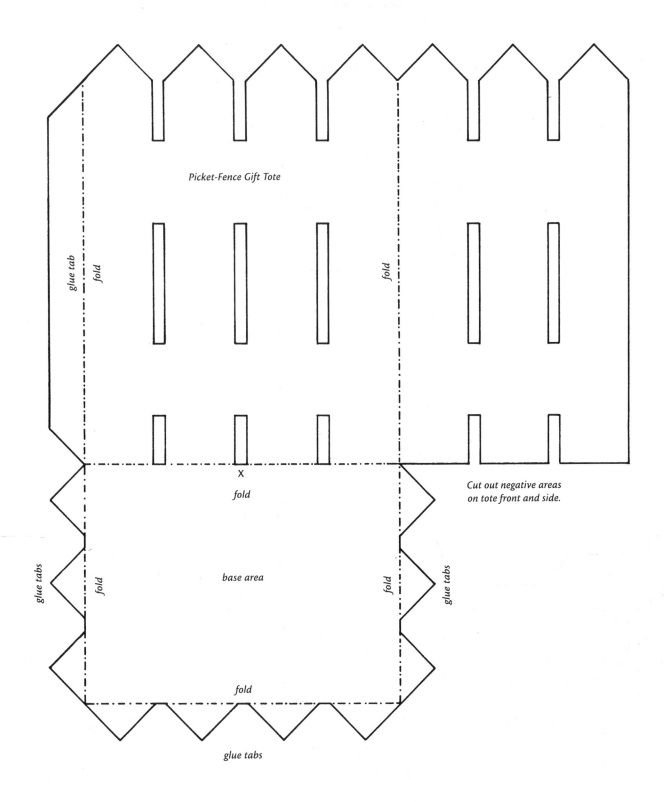

glue tab

fold

Picket-Fence Gift Tote

fold

X

fold

Cut out negative areas on tote front and side.

glue tabs

fold

base area

fold

glue tabs

fold

glue tabs

Pie Box

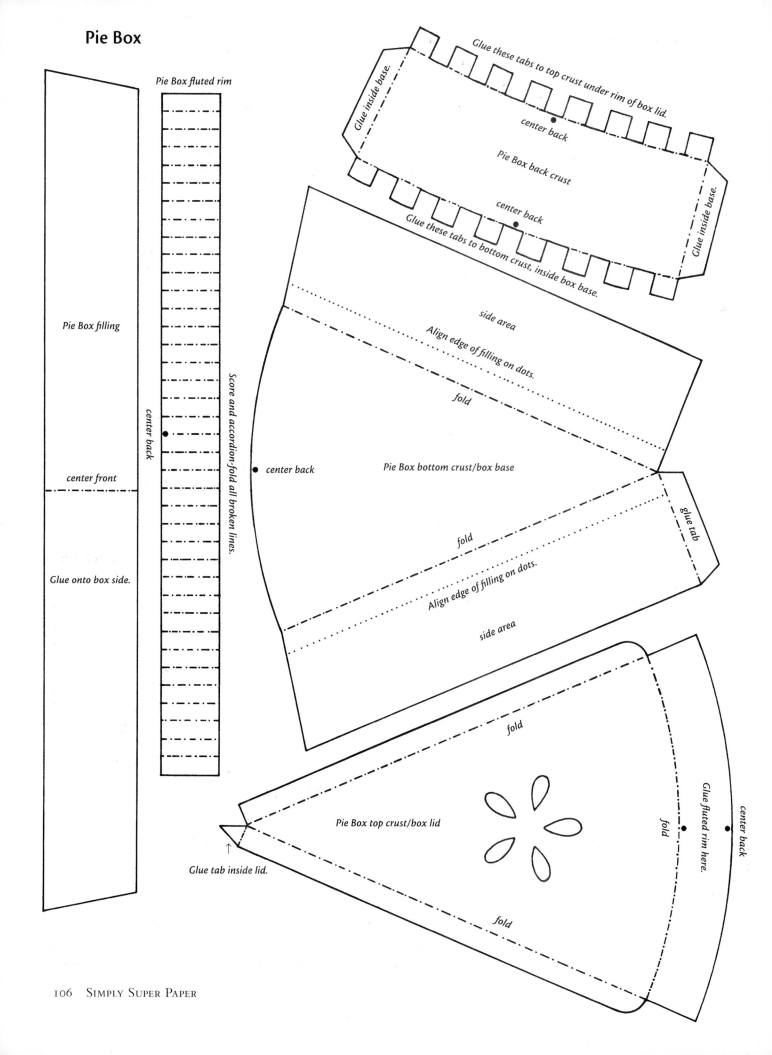

Pie Box fluted rim

Pie Box filling

center front

center back

Glue onto box side.

Score and accordion-fold all broken lines.

Glue these tabs to top crust under rim of box lid.

center back

Pie Box back crust

center back

Glue these tabs to bottom crust, inside box base.

Glue inside base.

Glue inside base.

side area

Align edge of filling on dots.

fold

center back

Pie Box bottom crust/box base

fold

Align edge of filling on dots.

side area

glue tab

fold

fold

fold

Glue fluted rim here.

center back

Pie Box top crust/box lid

Glue tab inside lid.

Birdhouse Gift Box

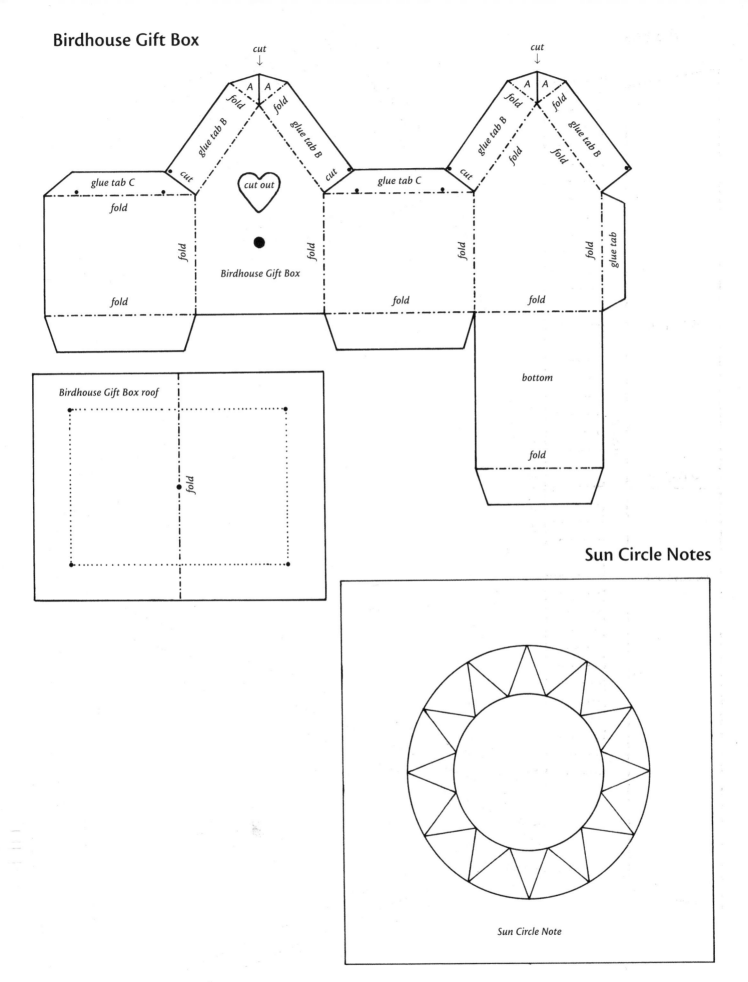

cut

A A

fold fold

glue tab B

glue tab B

cut

glue tab C

fold

fold

cut out

fold

Birdhouse Gift Box

glue tab C

cut

fold

cut

A A

fold fold

glue tab B

glue tab B

fold fold

fold

fold

glue tab

fold

bottom

fold

Birdhouse Gift Box roof

fold

Sun Circle Notes

Sun Circle Note

Star Basket

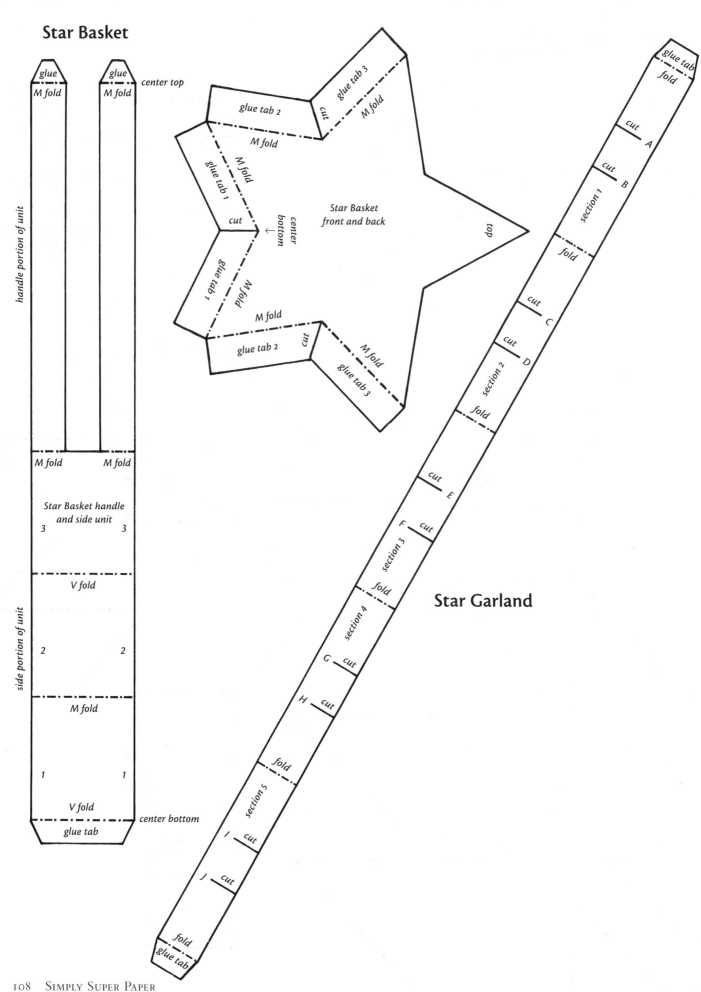

glue

M fold

glue

M fold

center top

handle portion of unit

glue tab 2

M fold

glue tab 1

M fold

M fold

cut

center bottom

M fold

M fold

cut

glue tab 3

M fold

top

Star Basket
front and back

glue tab 1

glue tab 2

cut

M fold

glue tab 3

M fold

M fold

M fold

Star Basket handle
and side unit

3

3

V fold

side portion of unit

2

2

M fold

1

1

V fold

center bottom

glue tab

glue tab

fold

cut

A

cut

B

section 1

fold

cut

C

cut

D

section 2

fold

cut

E

F

cut

section 3

fold

Star Garland

section 4

G

cut

H

cut

fold

section 5

I

cut

J

cut

fold

glue tab

Maple Leaf Projects

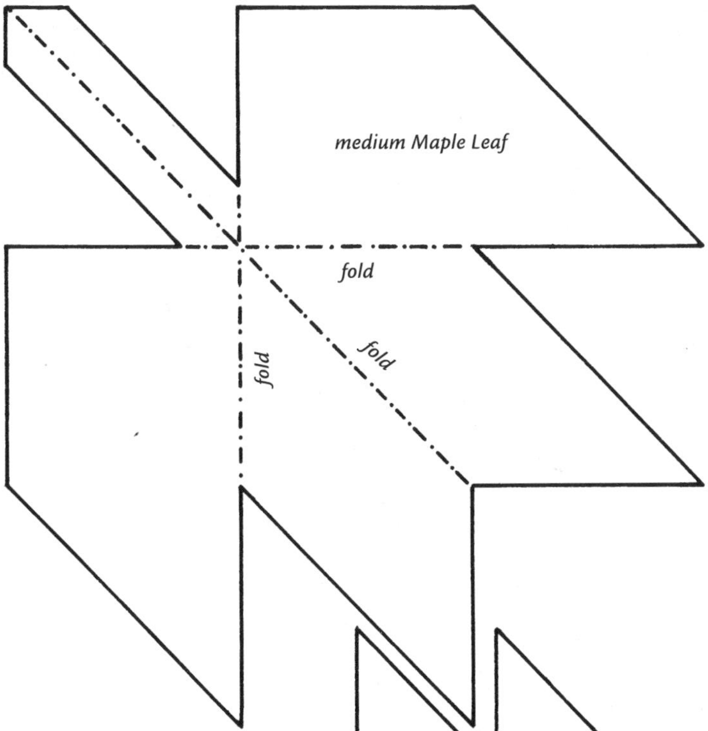

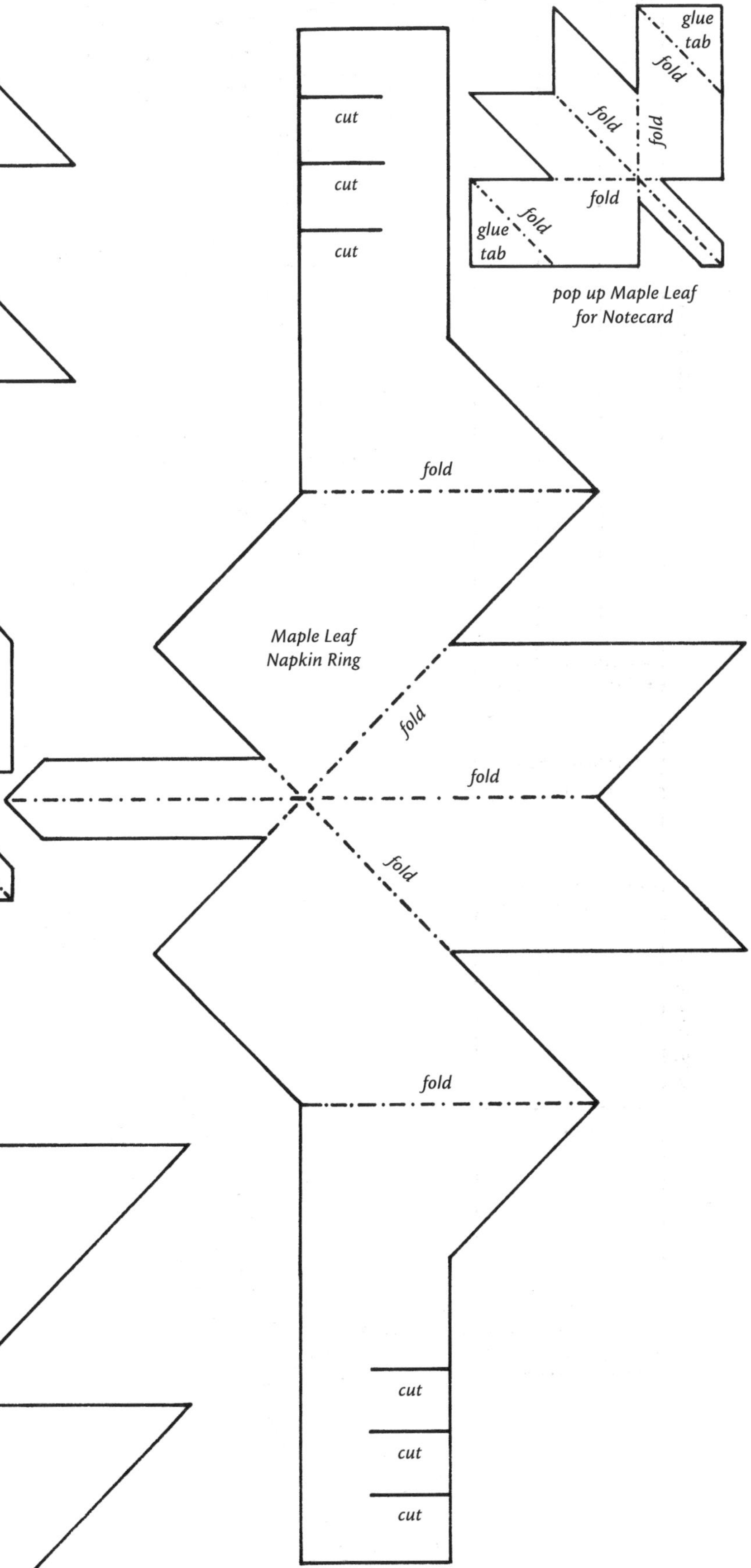

medium Maple Leaf

fold

fold

fold

small Maple Leaf

fold

fold

fold

Place on fold of paper for note card.

large Maple Leaf or
Maple Leaf Note Card

fold

fold

fold

cut

cut

cut

fold

Maple Leaf
Napkin Ring

fold

fold

fold

fold

cut

cut

cut

glue
tab

fold

fold

fold

fold

glue
tab

fold

pop up Maple Leaf
for Notecard

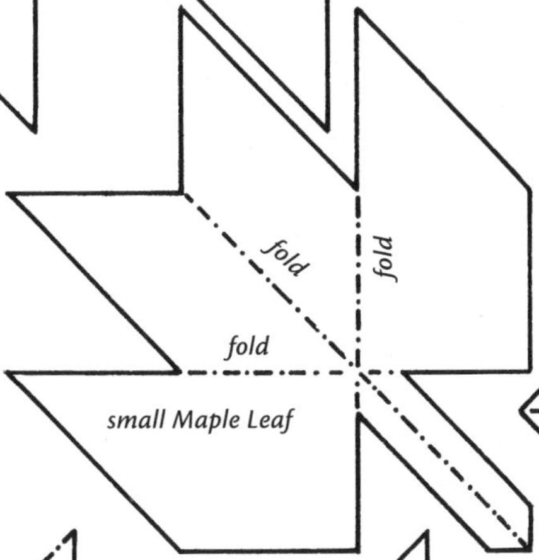

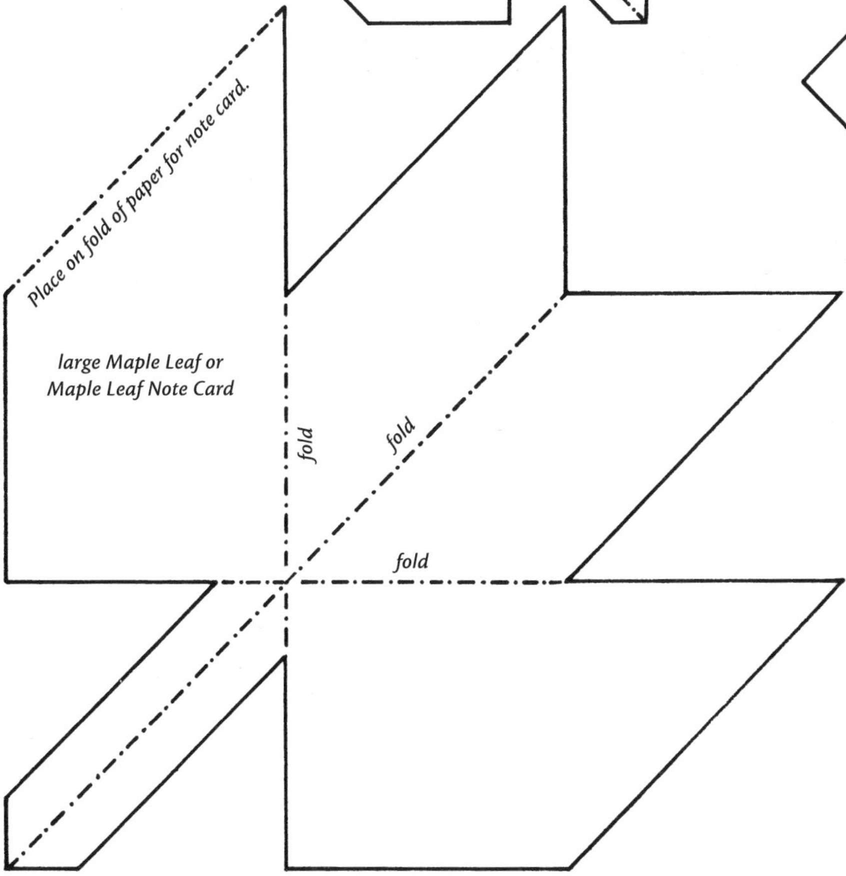

Quilter's Basket

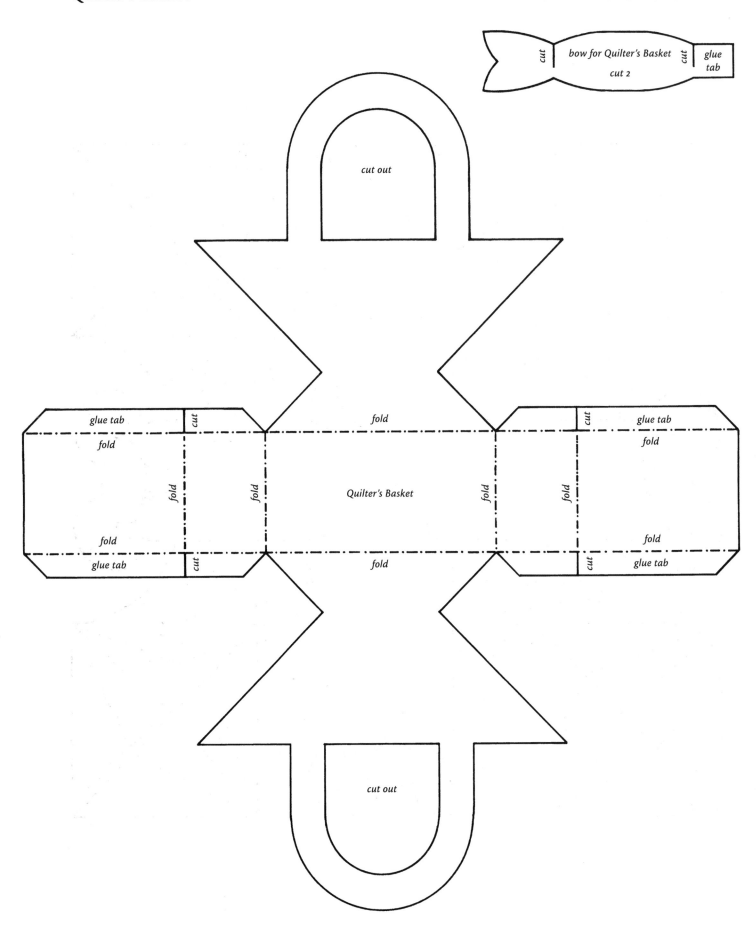

bow for Quilter's Basket
cut 2
cut
cut
glue tab

cut out

glue tab
fold
fold
fold
fold
glue tab

cut

cut

fold

Quilter's Basket

fold

fold
fold

glue tab
fold
fold
fold
glue tab

cut

cut

fold

cut out

Bat Pinwheel

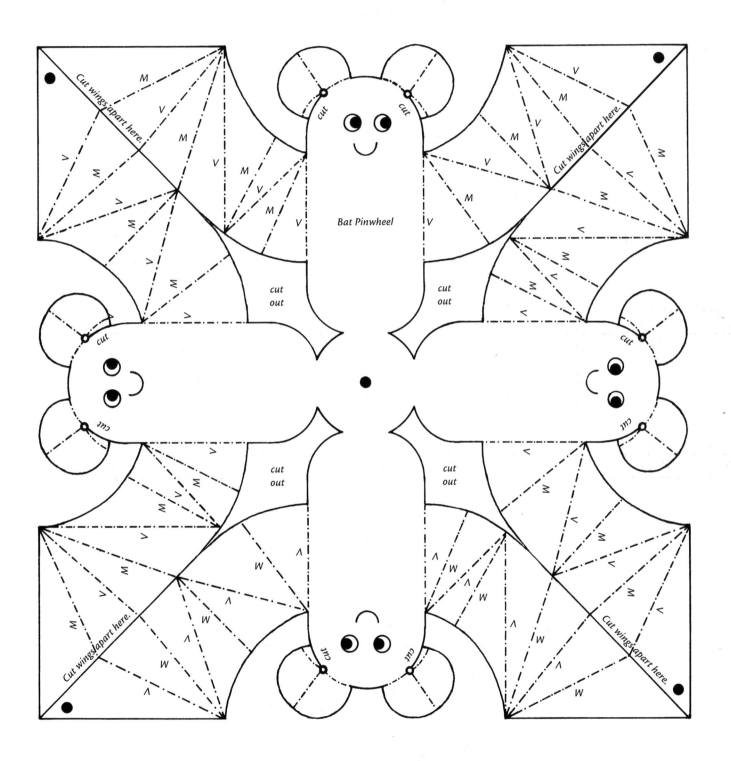

Bat Pinwheel

Ghost Pinwheel

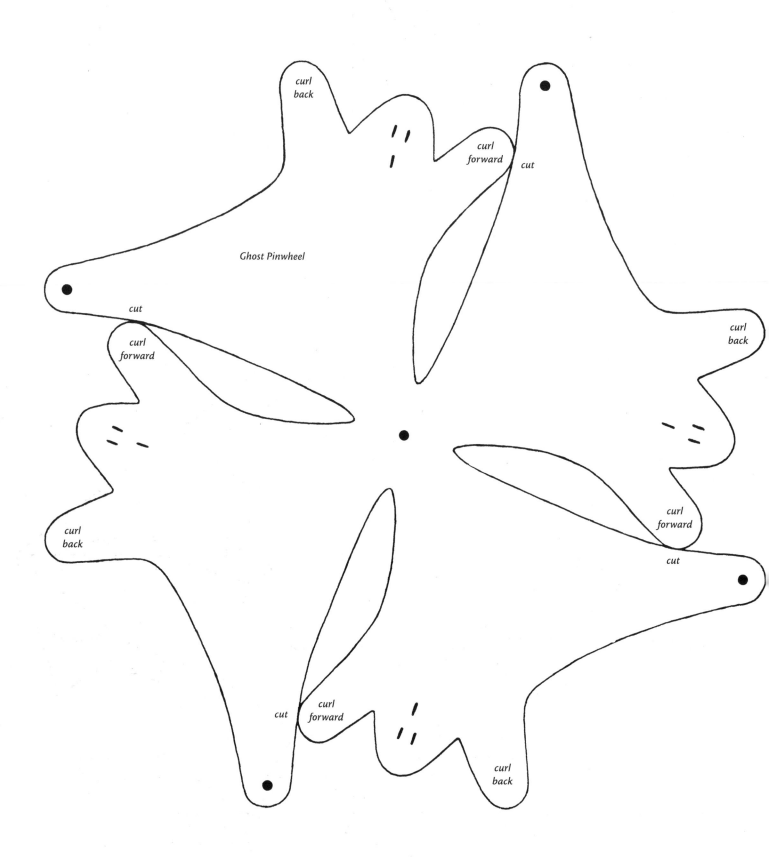

curl
back

curl
forward

cut

cut

curl
forward

Ghost Pinwheel

curl
back

curl
back

curl
forward

cut

curl
back

cut

curl
forward

cut

curl
back

Ghost Greeting Card and Garland

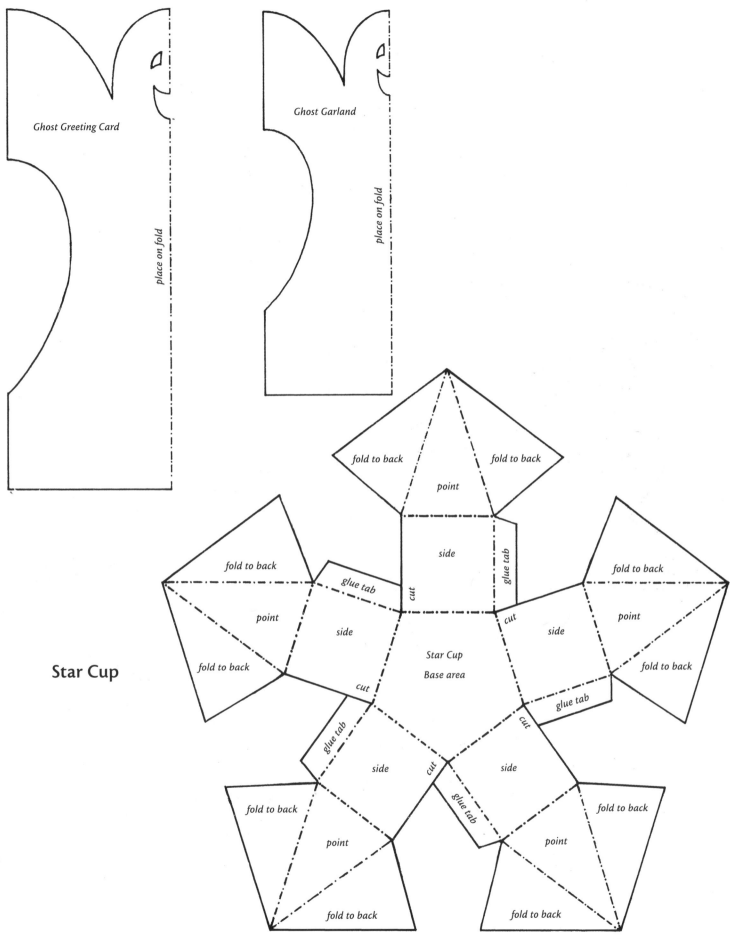

Ghost Greeting Card

place on fold

Ghost Garland

place on fold

Star Cup

fold to back

fold to back

point

side

glue tab

cut

fold to back

glue tab

point

side

cut

Star Cup
Base area

cut

side

glue tab

fold to back

point

side

cut

glue tab

fold to back

side

fold to back

point

fold to back

glue tab

side

point

fold to back

fold to back

fold to back

Good Witch

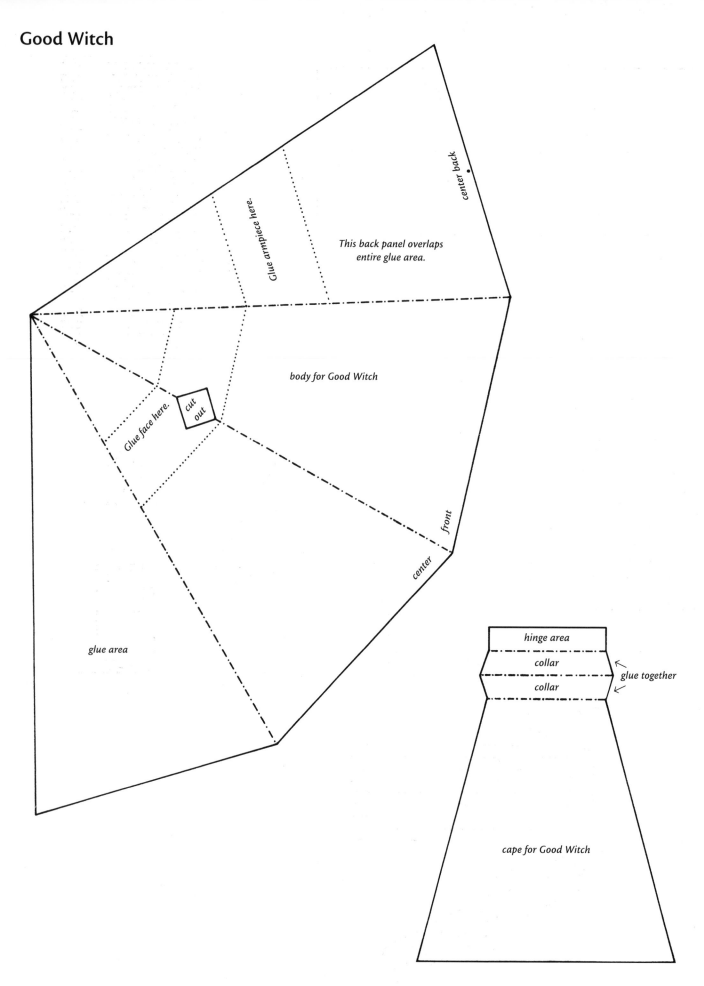

Glue armpiece here.

center back

This back panel overlaps
entire glue area.

body for Good Witch

Glue face here.

cut
out

center front

glue area

hinge area

collar

collar

glue together

cape for Good Witch

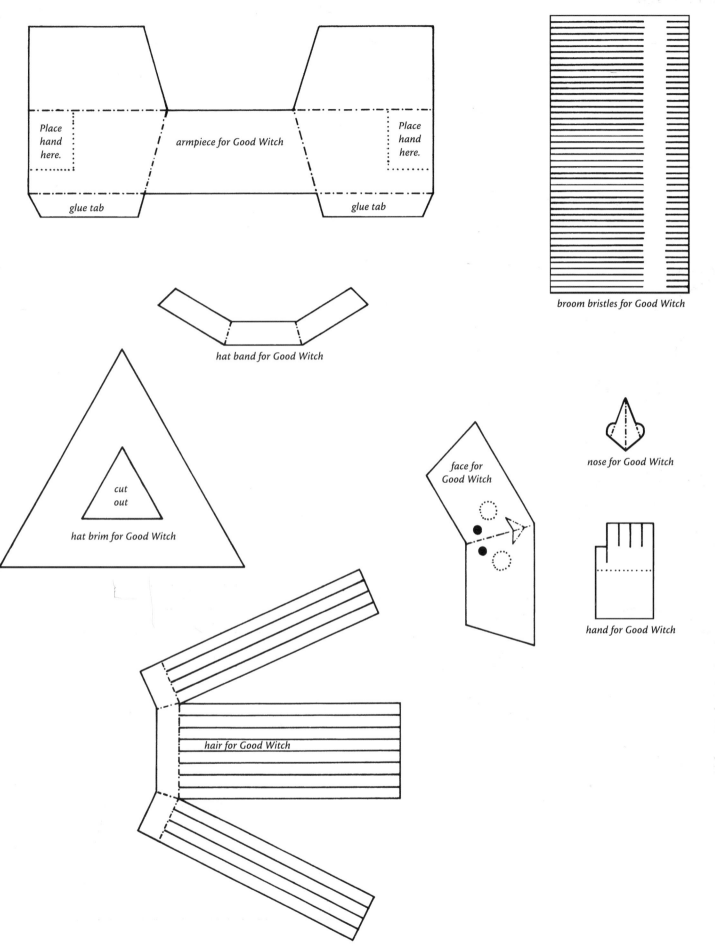

Place
hand
here.

armpiece for Good Witch

Place
hand
here.

glue tab

glue tab

broom bristles for Good Witch

hat band for Good Witch

cut
out

hat brim for Good Witch

face for
Good Witch

nose for Good Witch

hand for Good Witch

hair for Good Witch

Jack O' Lantern Baskets

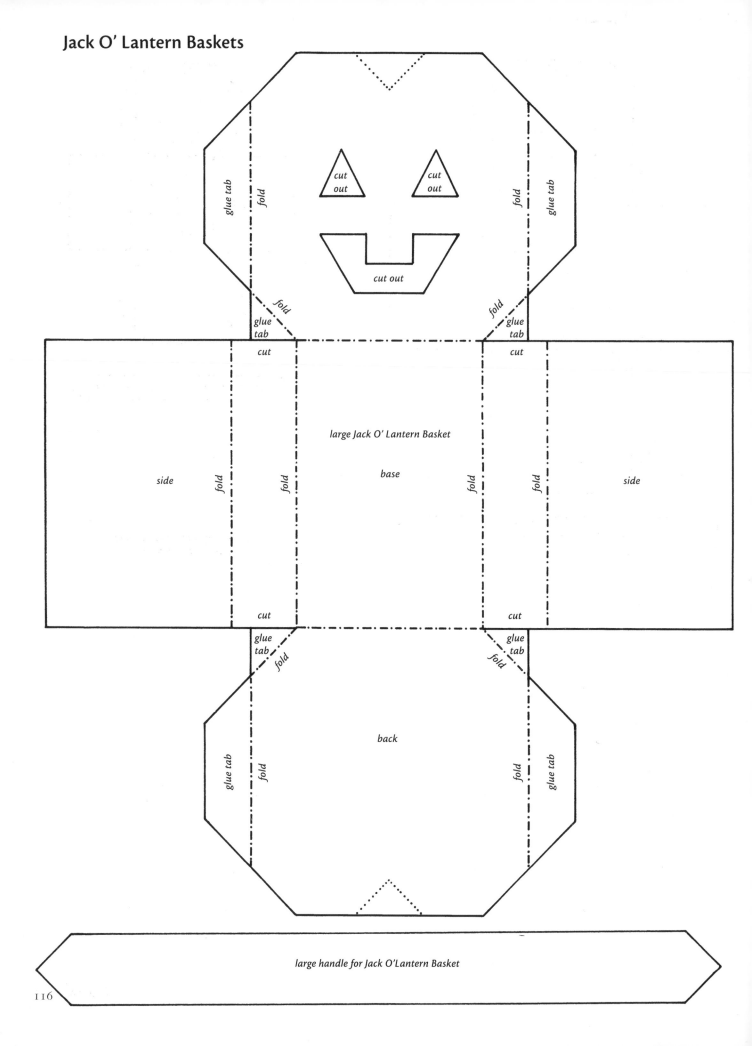

cut out

cut out

cut out

glue tab

fold

fold

glue tab

fold

glue tab

glue tab

fold

cut

cut

side

fold

fold

base

fold

fold

side

large Jack O' Lantern Basket

cut

cut

glue tab

fold

glue tab

fold

glue tab

fold

back

fold

glue tab

large handle for Jack O'Lantern Basket

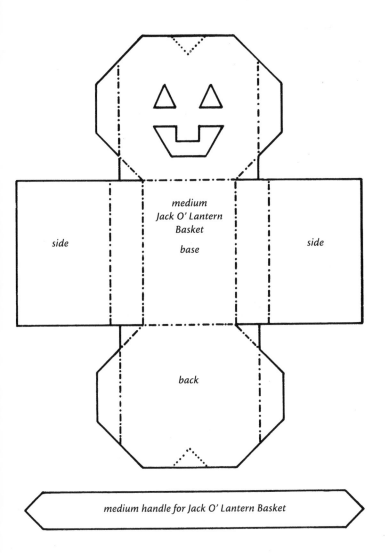

Jack O' Lantern

Basket

base

side

side

back

medium handle for Jack O' Lantern Basket

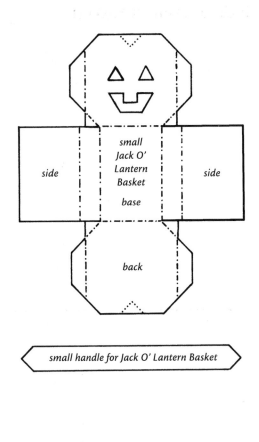

small
Jack O'
Lantern
Basket

base

side

side

back

small handle for Jack O' Lantern Basket

Follow labels as shown on large
Jack O' Lantern Basket.

Cottage Gift Boxes

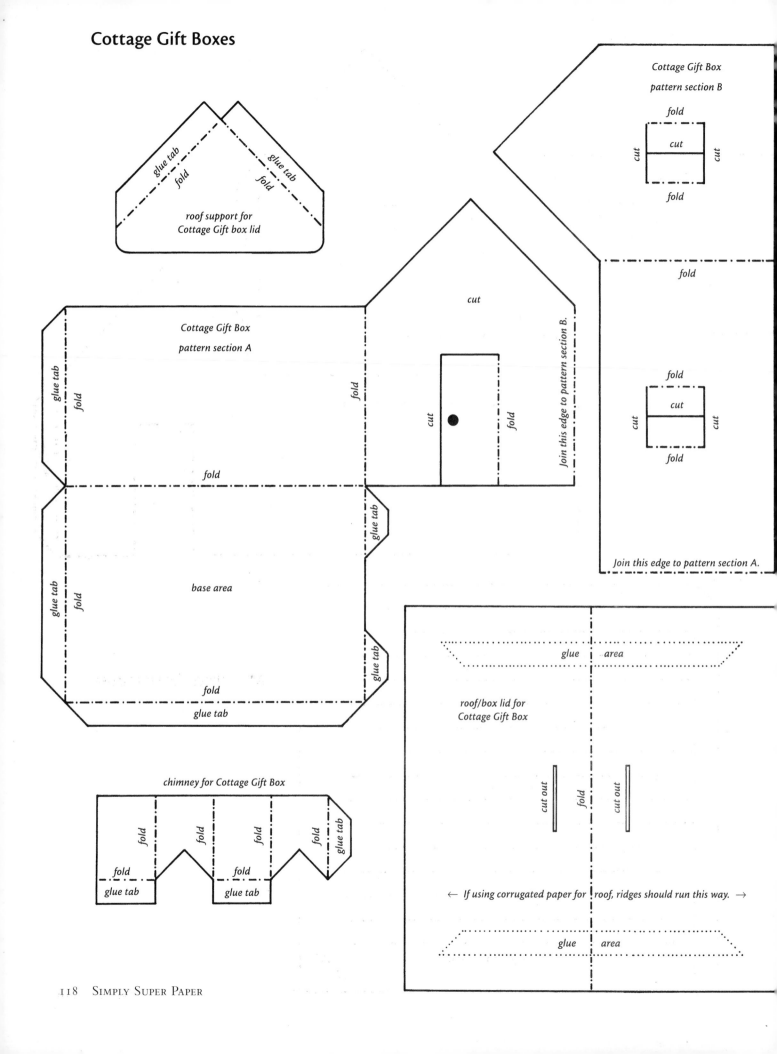

glue tab / fold

glue tab / fold

roof support for
Cottage Gift box lid

Cottage Gift Box
pattern section B

fold

cut

cut

cut

fold

glue tab

fold

Cottage Gift Box
pattern section A

fold

fold

cut

cut

fold

Join this edge to pattern section B.

fold

fold

cut

cut

cut

fold

base area

glue tab

fold

glue tab

glue tab

glue tab

fold

glue tab

Join this edge to pattern section A.

glue

area

roof/box lid for
Cottage Gift Box

cut out

fold

cut out

chimney for Cottage Gift Box

fold

fold

fold

fold

glue tab

fold

fold

glue tab

glue tab

← If using corrugated paper for roof, ridges should run this way. →

glue

area

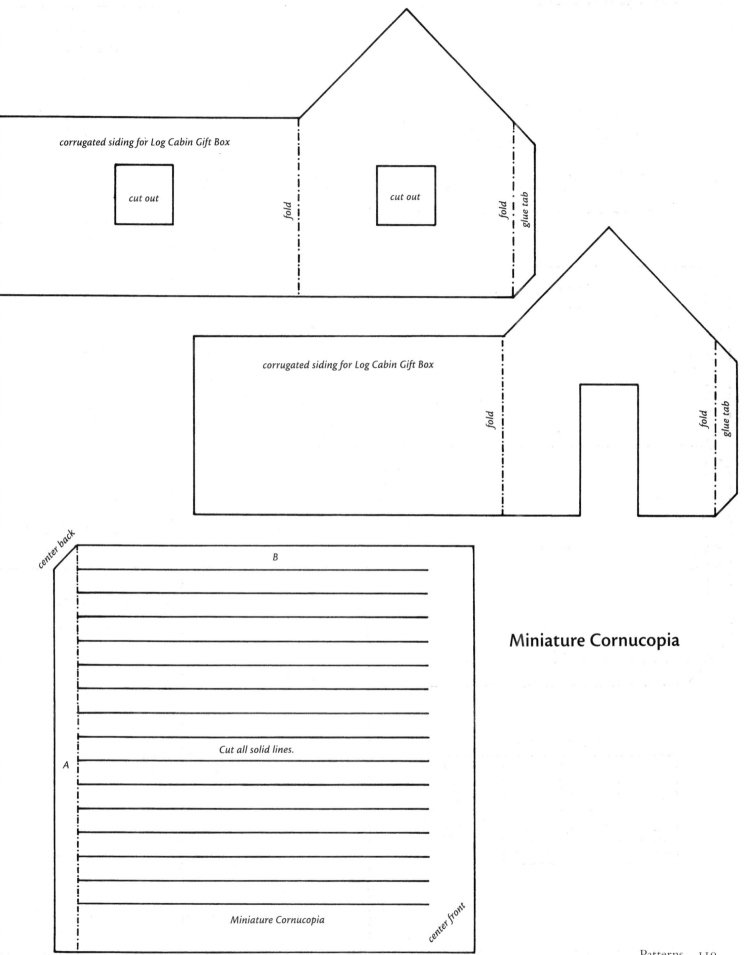

corrugated siding for Log Cabin Gift Box

cut out

cut out

fold

fold

glue tab

corrugated siding for Log Cabin Gift Box

fold

fold

glue tab

center back

B

Miniature Cornucopia

A

Cut all solid lines.

Miniature Cornucopia

center front

Standing Pine Tree

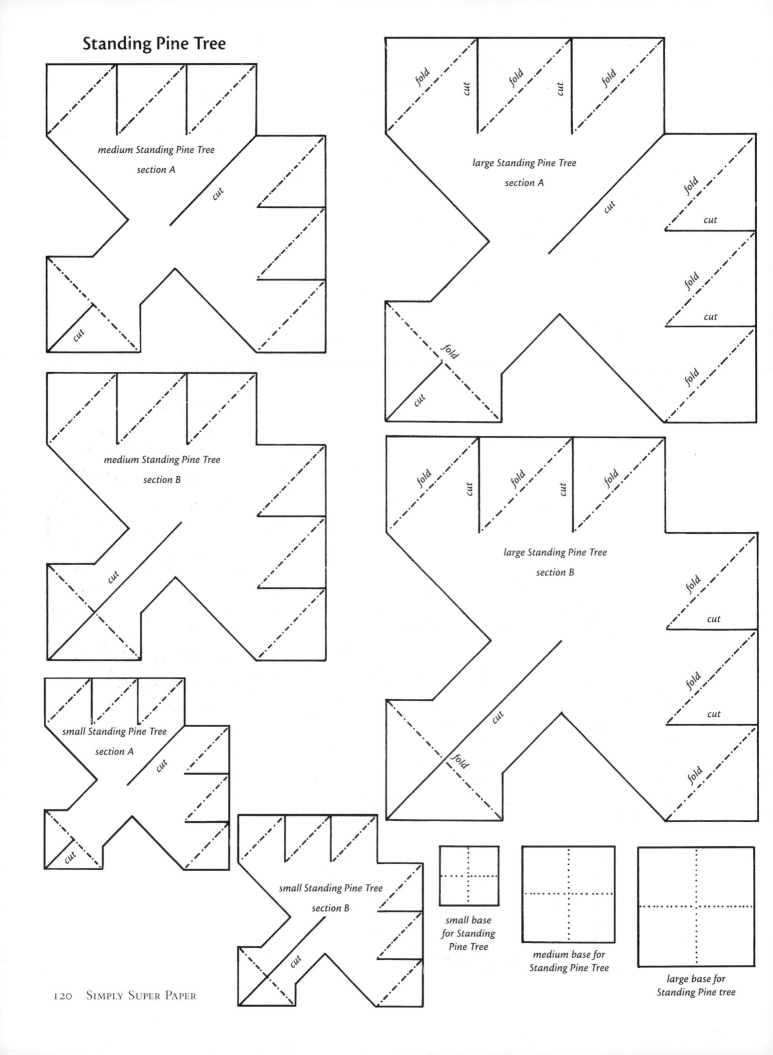

medium Standing Pine Tree
section A

cut

cut

large Standing Pine Tree
section A

fold *cut* *fold* *cut* *fold*

cut

fold

cut

fold

cut

fold

fold

cut

medium Standing Pine Tree

section B

cut

cut

large Standing Pine Tree

section B

fold *cut* *fold* *cut* *fold*

fold

cut

fold

cut

small Standing Pine Tree

section A

cut

cut

cut

cut

cut

fold

fold

cut

fold

cut

small Standing Pine Tree

section B

cut

small base
for Standing
Pine Tree

medium base for
Standing Pine Tree

large base for
Standing Pine tree

Shiny Stars

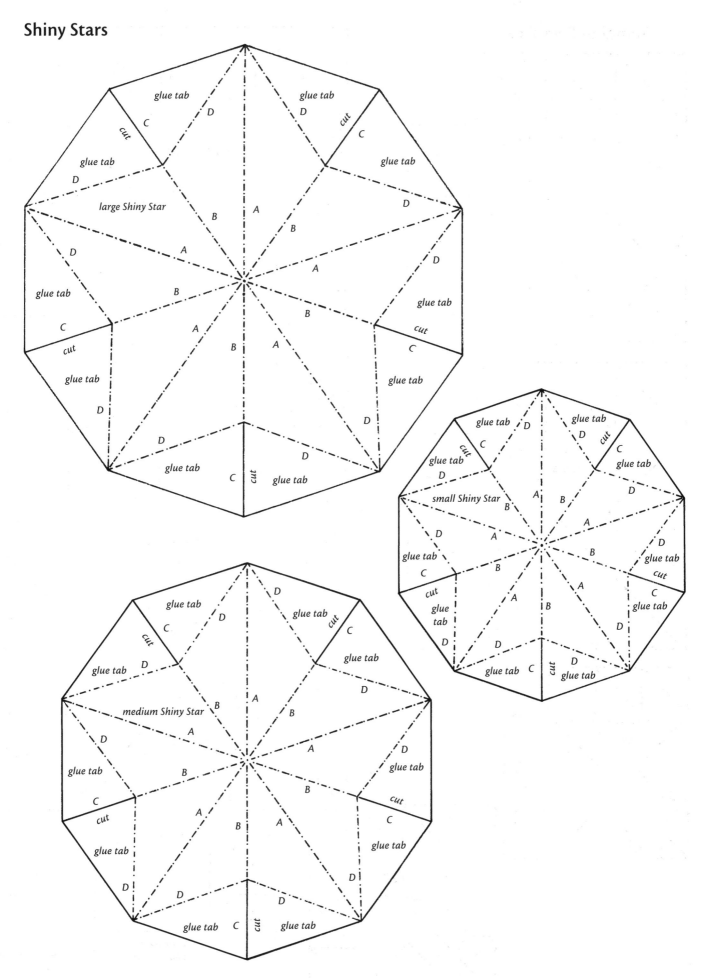

Snowflake Projects

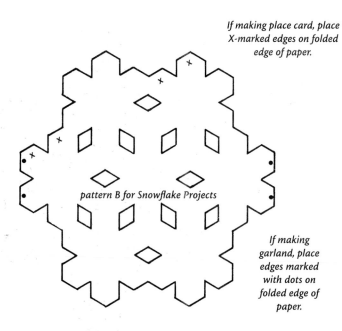

If making place card, place X-marked edges on folded edge of paper.

pattern B for Snowflake Projects

If making garland, place edges marked with dots on folded edge of paper.

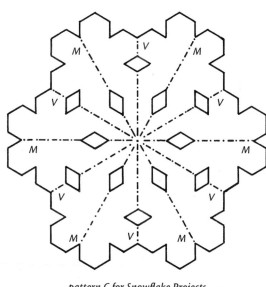

pattern C for Snowflake Projects

pattern A for Snowflake Projects

Little Glove Note

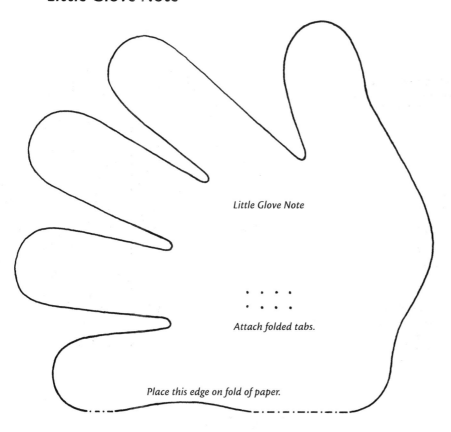

Little Glove Note

. . . .

Attach folded tabs.

Place this edge on fold of paper.

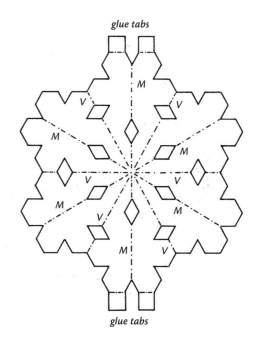

glue tabs

glue tabs

pop up snowflake for inside of
Little Glove Note

Folded Pine Tree Cards

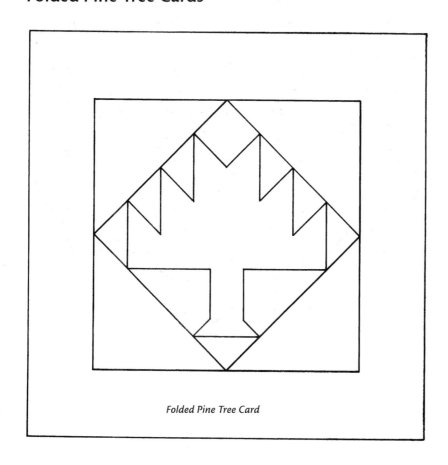

Folded Pine Tree Card

Snowman

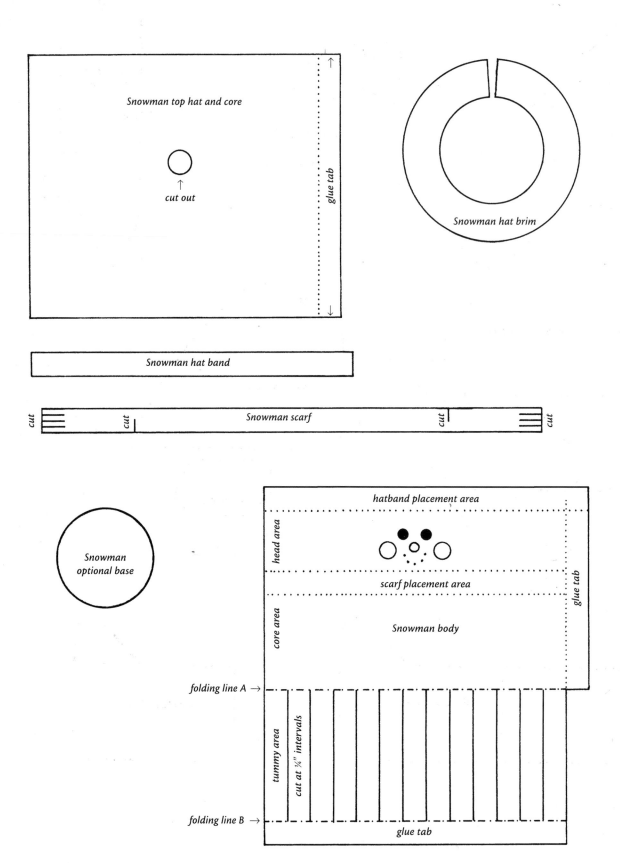

Snowman top hat and core

cut out

Snowman hat brim

Snowman hat band

cut   cut   Snowman scarf   cut   cut

Snowman optional base

hatband placement area

head area

scarf placement area

core area

Snowman body

glue tab

folding line A →

tummy area

cut at ¼" intervals

folding line B →

glue tab

Jointed Santa Card or Ornament

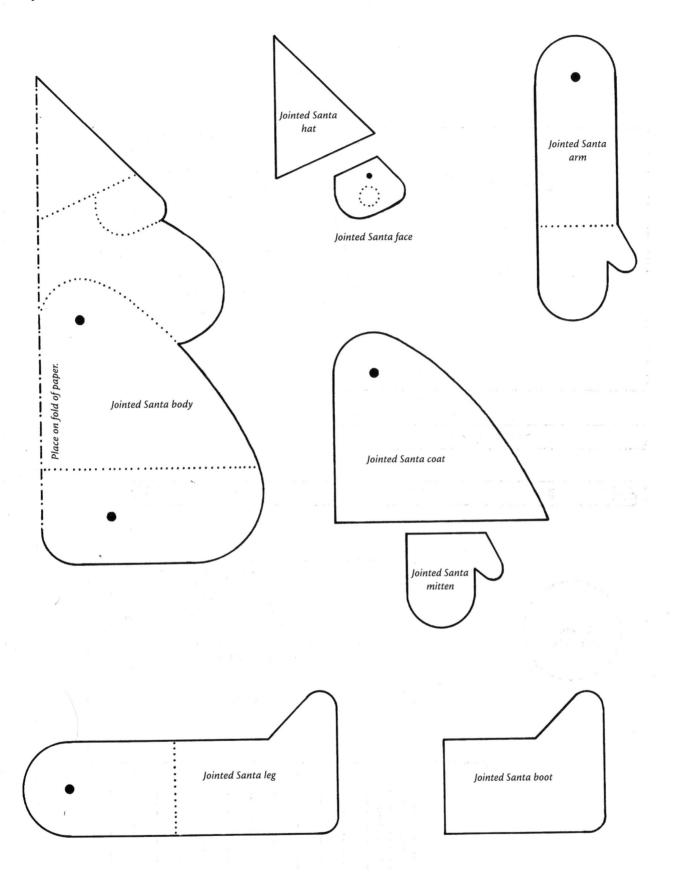

Jointed Santa hat

Jointed Santa face

Jointed Santa arm

Place on fold of paper.

Jointed Santa body

Jointed Santa coat

Jointed Santa mitten

Jointed Santa leg

Jointed Santa boot

Woven Coverlet Notes

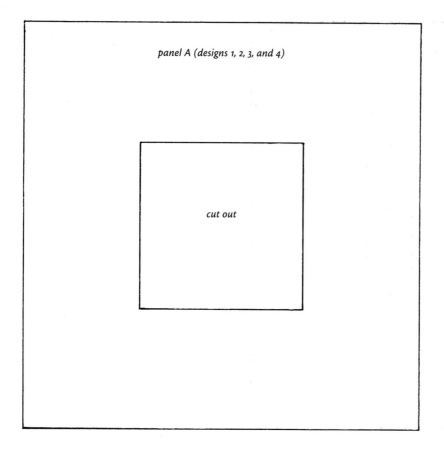

panel A (designs 1, 2, 3, and 4)

cut out

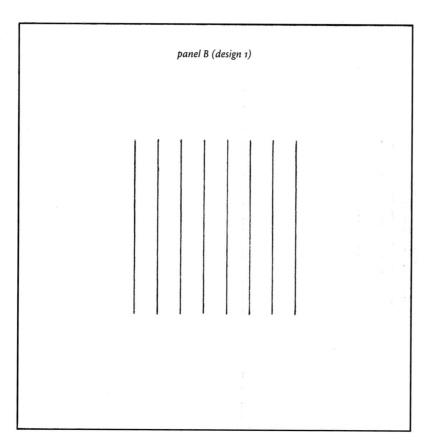

panel B (design 1)

Woven Coverlet Notes

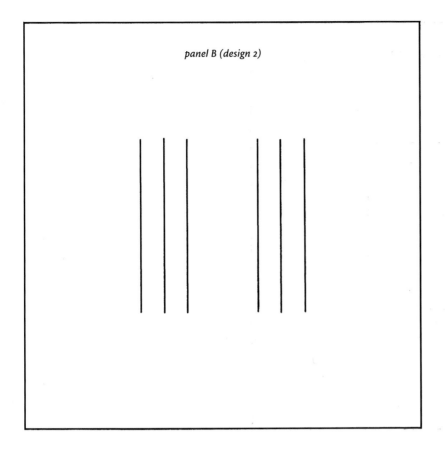

panel B (design 2)

panel B (design 3)

Woven Coverlet Notes

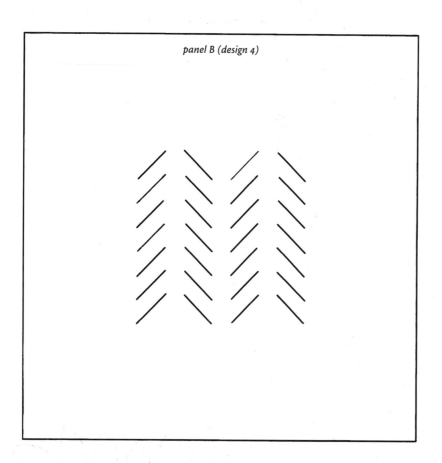

panel B (design 4)

Wreath Ornaments

heart for Holly Heart Wreath

Holly Heart Ornament

cut out

Feathered Wreath Ornament

cut out

Leaf and Berry Heart Ornament

cut out

Wreath Ornaments

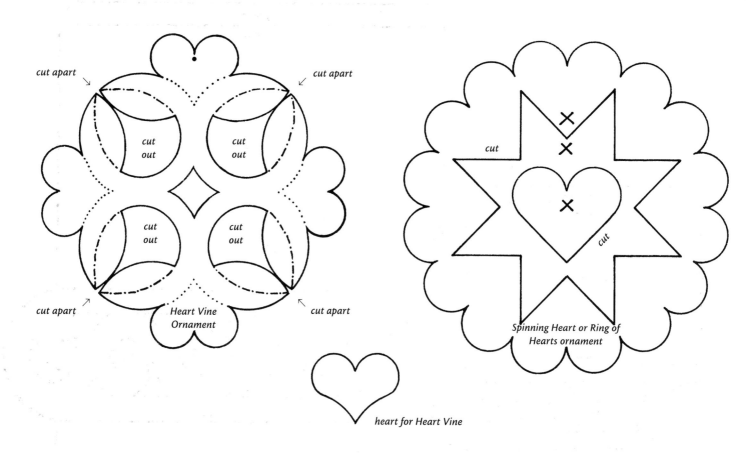

cut apart

cut apart

cut out

cut out

cut out

cut out

cut apart

cut apart

Heart Vine Ornament

cut

cut

Spinning Heart or Ring of Hearts ornament

heart for Heart Vine

Star Chain

cut

5-Point Star Chain

cut out

6-Point Star Chain

cut out

cut

Santa Sleigh

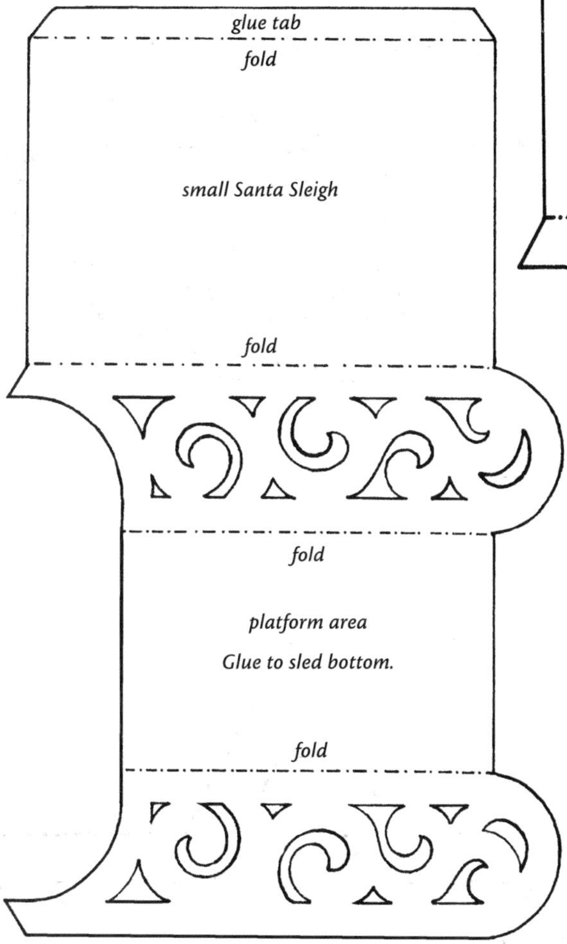

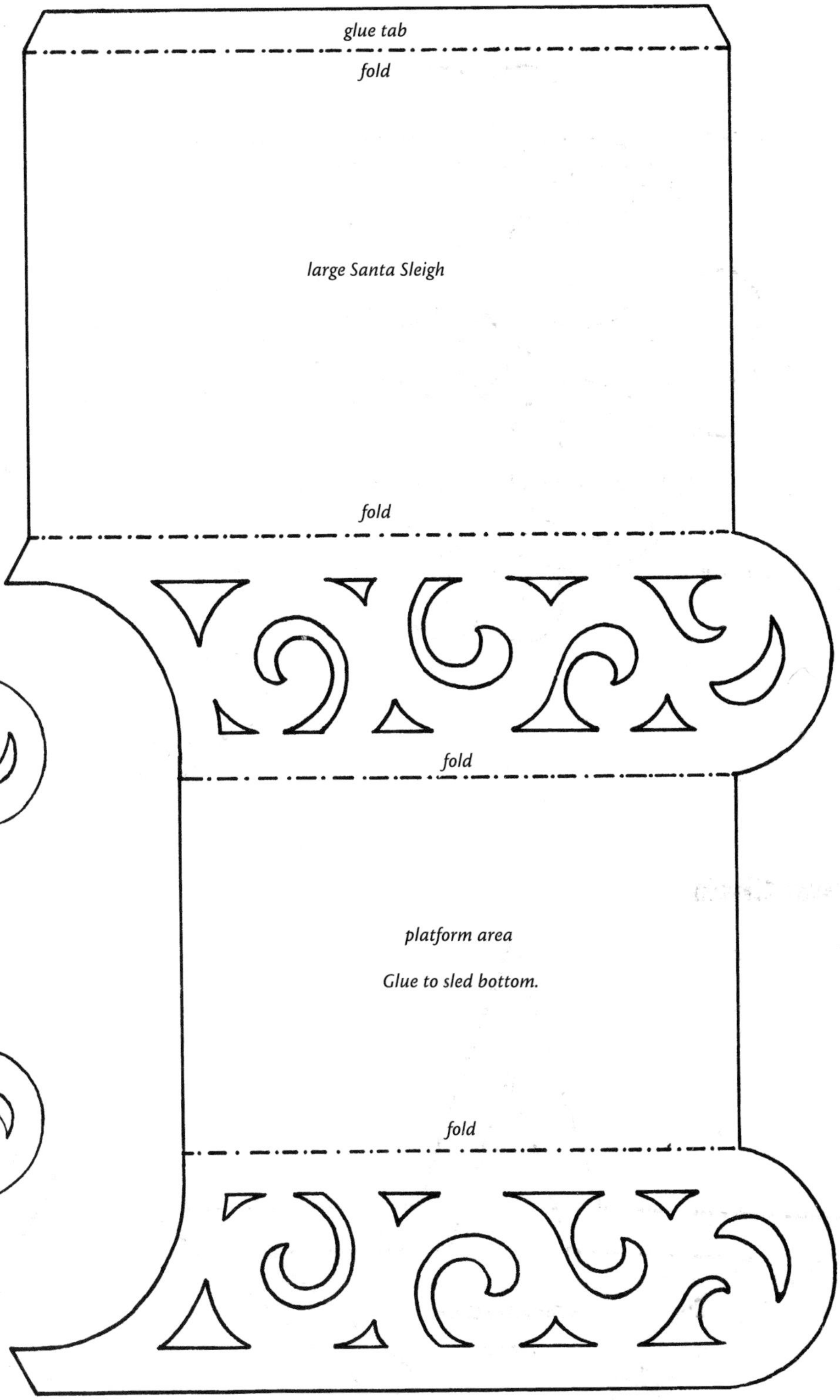

glue tab

fold

large Santa Sleigh

fold

fold

platform area
Glue to sled bottom.

fold

glue tab

fold

small Santa Sleigh

fold

fold

platform area
Glue to sled bottom.

fold

Santa Sleigh

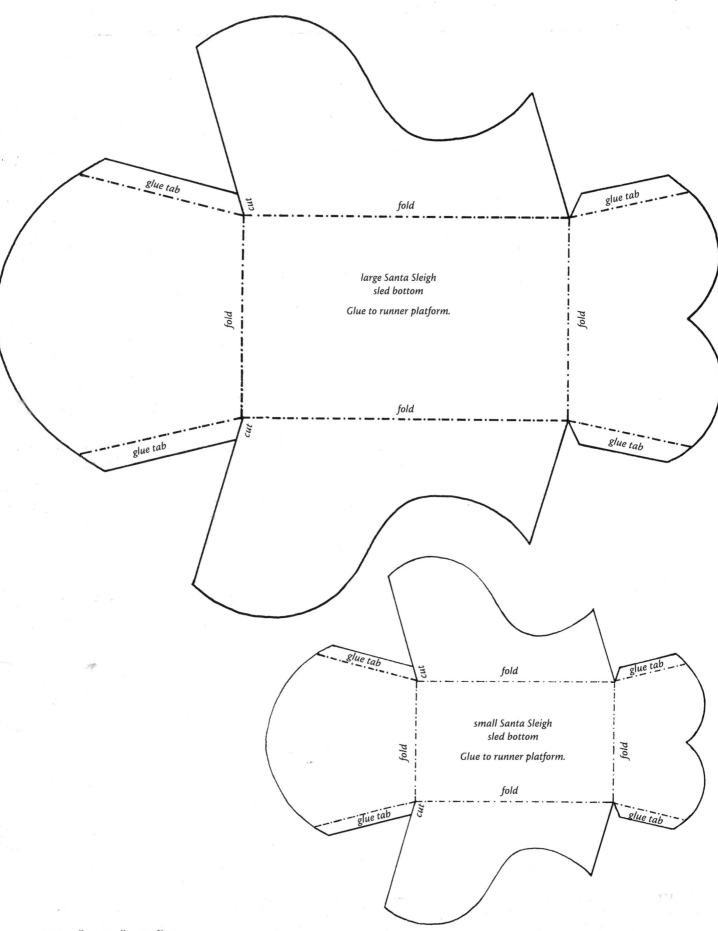

glue tab

fold

cut

fold

large Santa Sleigh
sled bottom

Glue to runner platform.

fold

fold

glue tab

cut

fold

glue tab

glue tab

fold

cut

fold

glue tab

small Santa Sleigh
sled bottom

Glue to runner platform.

fold

glue tab

cut

fold

glue tab